Train Your Brain

Puzzles

BOOK C

Challenging Puzzles
for Management Entrances; CAT, MAT, XAt etc

The First 'GRADED PUZZLE SERIES'

Train Your Brain

Puzzles

BOOK 

Challenging Puzzles

for Management Entrances; CAT, MAT, XAt etc

The First 'GRADED PUZZLE SERIES'

By
Terry Carter

Supported By
Sanmeen Kaur

ARIHANT PUBLICATIONS (INDIA) LIMITED

PRODUCTION TEAM
Publishing Manager : Amit Verma

Project Manager	:	Karishma Yadav	Cover Design	: Darin Zaidi
Project Coordinator	:	Divya Gusain	Layout & Design	: Shanu Mansoori
Project Reader	:	Reena Garg	Type Setting	: Vinay Sharma

For further information about the products from Arihant,
log on to www.arihantbooks.com *or email to* info@arihantbooks.com

Train Your Brain

Puzzles

BOOK C

Challenging Puzzles
for General Competition; Bank, SSC etc

The First 'GRADED PUZZLE SERIES'

CONTENTS

Let's Start to
TRAIN THE BRAIN

'Train Your Brain' Puzzles Book C contains different types of puzzles; Picture Puzzles, Math Puzzles, Word Puzzles, Logic Puzzles etc that will make you think logically. We assure that you will find your mind more streamlined, stretched & logical by the end of this book. Book C of this series has been especially prepared for the aspirants of Management Entrances (CAT, MAT, XAT etc) to sharpen their thinking skills and problem solving skills.

Through this book, we will be testing all the dimensions of your logical thinking abilities. The puzzles given here range from downright easy to essentially impossible. All the puzzles given in this book involve explicit or implicitly clearly defined procedures for solving them. Wherever required we have provided illustrations to help you understand the puzzle perfectly clear and understandable.

Although we have given the solutions at the end of the book but we advice you to 'Take the Challenge' and See! If you can figure out the puzzles before you look up the given explanations.

So push the boundaries of your thinking ahead and have fun solving these puzzles, one thing for sure-you will never be bored while solving these puzzles.

UNRAVEL THE MYSTERY

How to solve? There are many defined and undefined ways to solve a puzzle. The most sorted one is to have a list of facts that describe the information provided in the puzzles.

SOLVING LOGICAL PUZZLES

Step 1 **Analyzing the Puzzle** Always read the puzzles and clues given in it.

Step 2 **Arrangement of Information** Use the grid (table) as you find a information.

Step 3 **Compiling the Information** Read through the clues one at a time filling in what you discover as you go.

Step 4 **Extracting the Information** Look at the grid to discover what you can figure out now.

Step 5 **If still It Is Required** Review the puzzle and find clues, is there is still an unknown.

SOLVING MATHEMATICAL PUZZLES

Step 1 **Find and Use a Pattern** Identify a pattern, and then extend that pattern to solve the problem.

Step 2 **Build a Model** Use objects to represent the situation and the possible solutions.

Step 3 **Draw a Picture or Diagram** Show what is happening in the problem with a picture or a diagram.

Step 4 **Make a Table and/or a Graph** Organise and record your data in a table, chart, or graph. You are more likely to find a pattern or see a relationship when it is shown visually.

Step 5 **Write a Mathematical Sentence** If the problem involves numbers and number operations, a mathematical sentence or expression of a relationship with numbers or symbols, can help make the solution clearer.

Step 6 **Use Guess and Check, or Trial and Error** Even if a potential solution does not work, it may give you clues to other possibilities or help you to better understand the problem.

Step 7 **Break the Problem into Parts** If a problem is too large or complicated simplify it by breaking the problem into smaller and more manageable parts.

Step 8 **Work Backwards** Considering the goal first can make some problems easier. It helps you develop a strategy that leads to the solution by backing through the process.

Step 9 **Change Your Point of View** When a strategy is not working, discard what you are doing and try something else. This may help you think about the problem in a different way.

Puzzles

1.

Consider the following diagram.

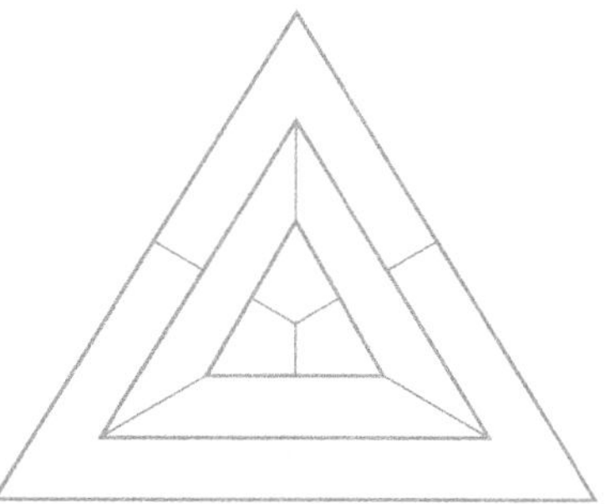

What is the minimum number of colours required to fill the spaces in the diagram without any two adjacent spaces having the same colour?

2.

A survey was conducted by a private survey company to know the traits of the candidates who appear for IIT-JEE entrance exam. Below is given a figure with four intersecting circles, each representing a group of the persons having the quality written against it. You are required to find the region which represents the people who are not enterprising, studious and disciplined but are very laborious?

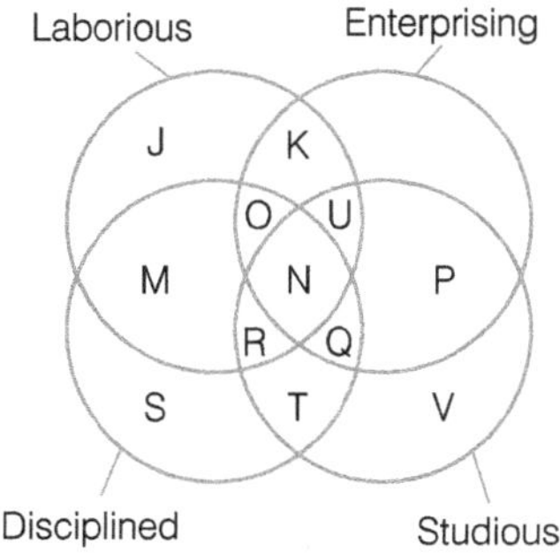

3.

A boy was carrying a basket of eggs. He fell down and all the eggs broke. When he went back home without any egg, his mother asked how many he had been carrying altogether in the basket. He was unable to remember.

But he was able to recall that when they were counted two at a time one was left, when counted three at a time one was left, when counted four at a time one was left, when counted five at a time none was left.

Can you tell how many eggs were broken?

4.

Pablo Picasso is a world renowned artist, made 4 master pieces (1), (2), (3) and (4) and asked one of his appreciators to find the image (X), inscribed in these 4 figures.

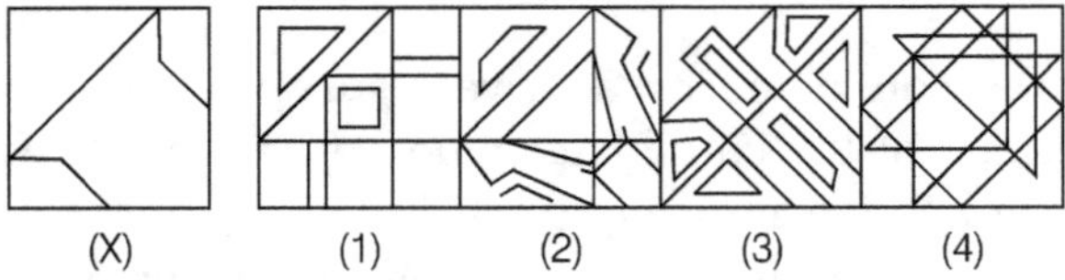

Can you help appreciator of Picasso's painting to find the original master piece?

5.

Some terrorists planned a bomb in Central Park, Delhi and used a unique method of its explosion. They have used a telephone as detonator whose one number disappear each minute. To dispose this bomb Major Samar Anand of Indian Army was called and he cut exactly the wire, which could have exploded the bomb in the five minutes. The numbers which appeared were as follows:

1st minute	2nd minute	3rd minute	4th minute	5th minute
589654237	89654237	8965423	965423	?

What could have been the number, if Major Samar Anand have not cut the exact wire to avoid explosion?

6.

Sean caught a prize fish last weekend. He was going to measure it but realised that his ruler was not long enough. He was able to measure the head and discovered that it was 9 cm long, he then measured the tail and found that it was the length of the head plus half the length of the body. If the body was the length of the head plus the tail, what is the total length of the fish?

7.

Bravo Dicosta, a famous French fashion designer, was famous for his cut work designs on long dresses and gowns. For the Paris fashion week, he decided a theme on universe and made different pictures of cut work design samples on papers to be used on the gowns. He kept the samples intact in packets with a colour similar to the colour of the dress. One of his packets got misplaced and got into the hands of his competitor designer. He tried to understand the design from the picture to copy for his collection. Can you find what design was made by designer Bravo?

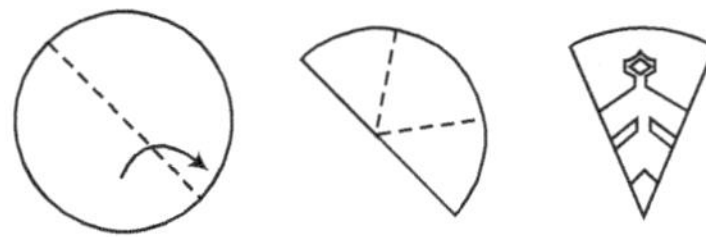

Cut work design pattern

8.

Indian Parliament has very unique security system and any member, who wants to reach the central hall has to go through four stage security system, which has been presented below.

Stage 1	2	20	58	131	254	?
Stage 2	18	38	73	123	?	
Stage 3	20	35	50	?		
Stage 4	15	15				

Can you tell us what were the codes at third stage of security check?

9.

A car parking lot at Udyog Bhawan can accommodate only 6 cars. The 6 cars are parked in 2 rows in such a way that the front of the 3 cars parked in row 1 is facing the other 3 cars in other row.

   (i) Alto is not parked in the beginning of any row.

 (ii) Esteem is second to the right of i10.

(iii) Punto, who is the neighbour of Alto is parked diagonally opposite to i10.

(iv) Swift is parked in front of Alto.

 (v) SX4 is parked to the immediate right of Alto.

If SX4 and Esteem exchange their positions mutually, then which car is adjacent to Esteem?

10.

Consider the following diagram.

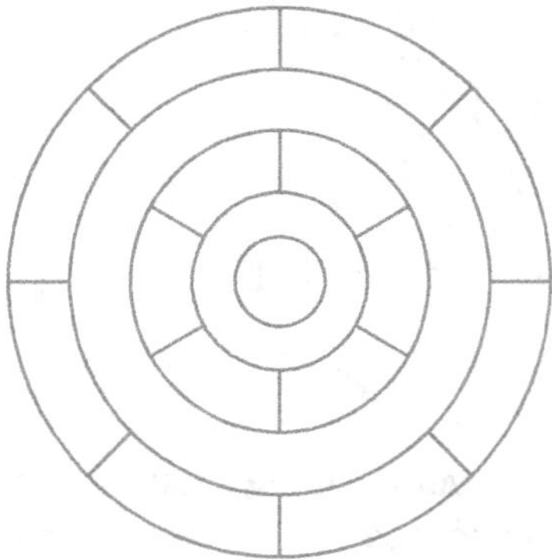

What is the minimum number of different colours required to paint the figure given above such that no two adjacent regions have the same colour?

11.

Practicing decoding number sequences also hones your numerical logic. Artist Istvan has made a third number zone installation, this time at an outdoor festival. Two tickets to the main stage are offered to the person who can decide which of the five sets of numbers a-e should be used for the fourth screen in the number zone. You have to identify the coded sequence Istvan sets up in the first three sets of nine numbers.

3	11	15		8	16	20		13	21	25		
18	24	32		15	21	29		12	18	26		?
22	21	9		26	25	13		30	29	17		

18	26	30		16	31	30		18	26	30		16	26	32		13	26	30
10	15	22		10	15	23		9	15	23		9	15	23		9	15	22
34	31	22		34	33	21		34	33	21		34	31	22		34	33	22

| (a) | (b) | (c) | (d) | (e) |

12.

Mr. Pollack is a great gambler. One day he went to casino in Las Vegas where he saw different rolling dice games were being played. He went to a table on which two six sided dice are being rolled where he bid on getting a total of 7 whose probability of coming was $\frac{1}{6}$. He wins the game on table 1.

He then went to try his luck on the different tables where 7 sided, 8 sided, 9 sided and 10 sided dice were rolled, but he choose to bid on getting a total of 7 only. Now, what would be his probability of winning on these tables?

13.

Following a logical pattern, complete this puzzle.

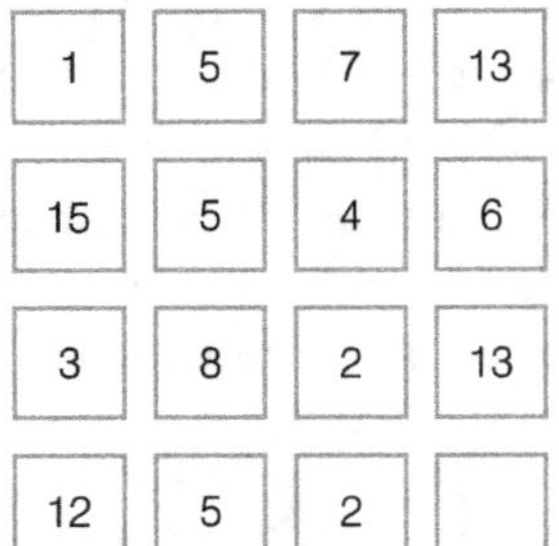

14.

Which of the bottom numbers goes in the centre circle?

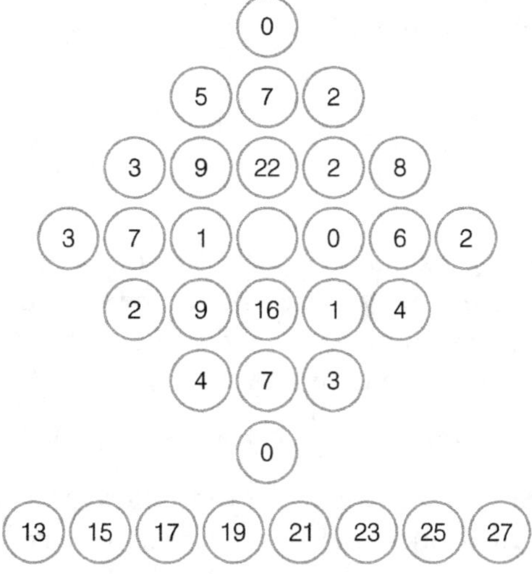

15.

Addison's father Mr. Daewon was suffering from Amnesia i.e. short term memory loss. While going for a business meeting Mr. Daewon choose to go on his car to save himself from getting late. On coming back from the venue of his business meeting, he forgot to take his car and came back home on train. Addison on realising it asked his father about the place where he parked the car. Being a patient of Amnesia Mr. Daewon could only recapitulate a part of the design made on the building of the hotel where his meeting held. Going through all the hotels near by the place. Addison could sort out four hotels matching the part of the design that his father told him. Out of these four hotels' designs help Addison to find out where his father's meeting took place.

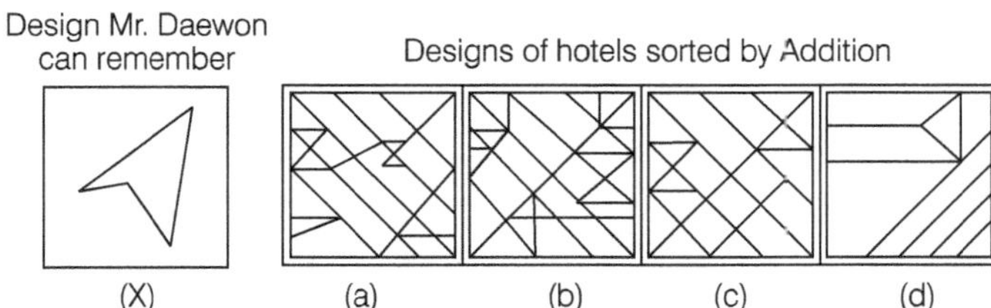

16.

After the Kalka Mail Derailment following statements, conclusions and possibilities of happening were issued by Railway Minister.

Statement I   Kalka Express met with an accident.

Statement II The body of the driver was not recovered.

Conclusion I Driver died in the accident.

Conclusion II Driver escaped in the accident.

Possibility I   Only conclusion I follows.

Possibility II Only conclusion II follows.

Possibility III Either conclusion I or II follows.

Possibility IV Neither conclusion I nor II follows.

Based upon the above notice, which possibility do you think is valid?

17.

Few days ago, I was at New Delhi railway station to receive my cousion. I went to the railway enquiry counter and asked about the running status of the train. But the four representatives of railway sitting over there were talking in the manner which could not be understood by the common men. The 1st representative said, 'Min Fin Bin Gin' means 'trains are always late'; 2nd representative said, 'Gin Fin Cin Hin' means 'drivers are always punished'. The 3rd representative said, 'Bin Cin Vin Rin' means 'drivers stopped all trains'. The 4th representative said, 'Min Kin Fin Vin' means 'all passengers are late'.

After listening to this conversation, can you say what does 'Hin Fin Kin' mean in their language?

18.

Which of the bottom squares fits logically at the end of this puzzle?

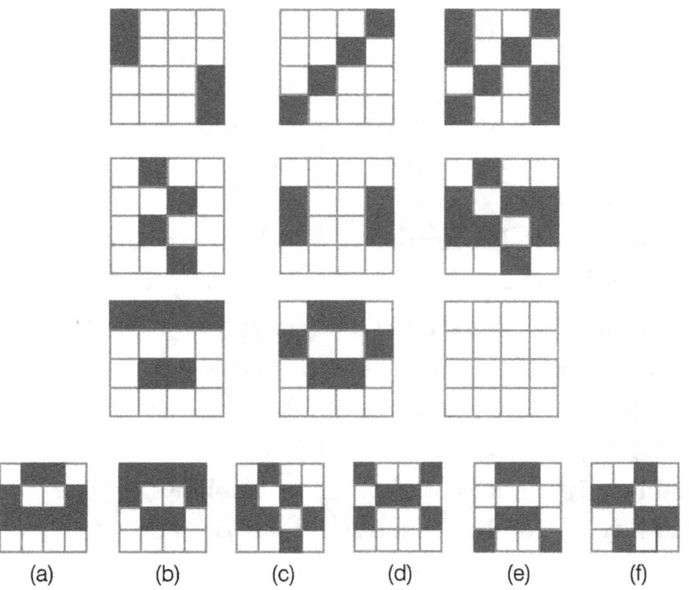

(a)   (b)   (c)   (d)   (e)   (f)

19.

This puzzle will test your imagination.

If we tie a sheep to one peg, it eats out a circle in grass. If we put a rope through a ring on its neck and tie both ends of the rope to two pegs, it eats out an ellipse. If we want an oval we tighten one rope between two pegs put a ring with a rope on it and tie the sheep to its other end.

How to tie a sheep so that it eats out a square in grass? We have one sheep, ropes, pegs and rings.

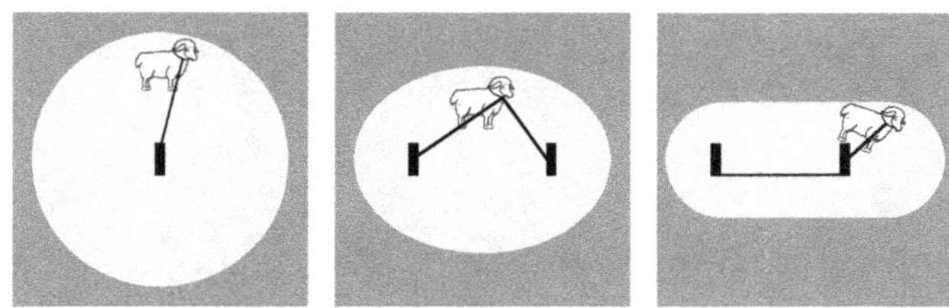

20.

Which of the bottom six grids completes this pattern?

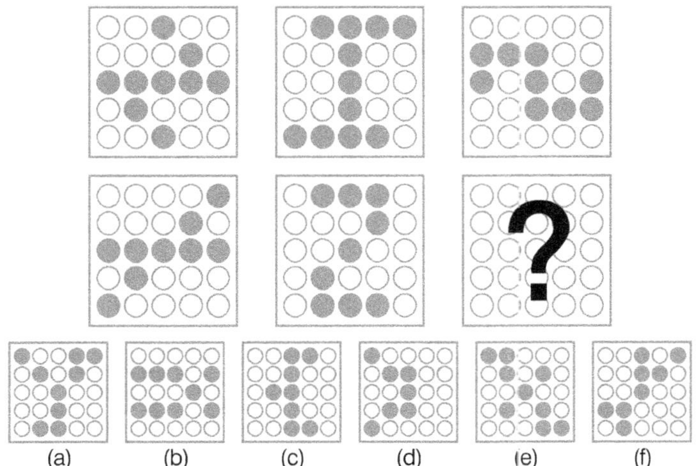

(a)	(b)	(c)	(d)	(e)	(f)

21.

2	16	10	1	8	− 7
10	?	?	?	?	1
33	?	?	?	?	24
17	?	?	?	?	8
15	?	?	?	?	6
34	48	42	33	40	25

Which is the missing section?

(a)

24	17	8	16
46	41	30	38
32	25	15	24
29	22	13	20

(b)

23	18	9	15
47	39	30	38
31	24	15	23
27	22	14	21

(c)

23	17	8	15
46	39	32	39
32	24	16	24
27	23	13	20

(d)

24	18	9	16
47	41	32	39
31	25	16	23
29	23	14	21

22.

Four married couples: Agatha and John, Barbara and Kevin, Celine and Leon, and Daphne and Matthew (the hosts) were celebrating Matthew's birthday. Everybody was sitting at a round table in such a way that each lady was seated between two gentlemen and all the couples were separated. Agatha took her seat between Kevin and Matthew. Matthew sat to the right of Agatha. John was sitting next to Daphne. Who took the seat to the right of Barbara?

23.

In the G-8 meeting at Kuala Lumpur, representatives A, B, C, D, E, F, G and H from 8 different countries *viz.* Thailand, France, Holland, Austria, US, Spain, India and Germany (not necessarily in the same order) sit around a circular table facing the centre. A, who represents Germany, sits 3rd to the left of E. The one, who is from India sits on the immediate right of A. D who is from Holland, sits 2nd to the right of B. B is not an immediate neighbour of E. C, who is from Spain, sits exactly in the middle of people representing US and India. G, the representative from France, sits 2nd to the left of H, who is from Thailand.

Can you determine the representative from which country is seated 2nd to the left of the Indian representative?

24.

Subhash Ghai, a film producer and director has selected five places for shooting in Himachal Pradesh namely Shimla, Kullu, Manali, Dharamshala and Mandi. The distance between any two of these places in the kilometre is as follows:

	Shimla	Kullu	Manali	Dharamshala	Mandi
Shimla	0	2	3	5	6
Kullu		0	2	1	4
Manali			0	2	3
Dharamshala				0	2
Mandi					0

Subhash Ghai is currently in Dharamshala and wants to finish his shooting at Mandi. If he does not want to visit a city more than once, what is the minimum distance he would have to cover?

25.

Business is booming in the 'Sunset Vue' bar, where the customers really enjoy the 'Make A Sum' game that barman and philosophy student Carlo sets up for them with the coasters. Here's another chance to play. Carlo has laid out the number coasters as below and you have to make a working sum by inserting the four mathematical symbols (+, −, ÷, ×) between the coasters shown. The symbols can be in any order.

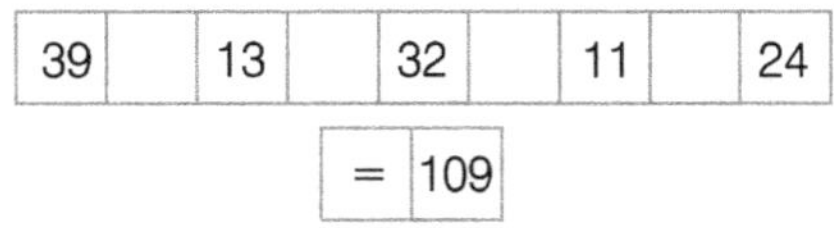

26.

In Delhi, there are three bus routes: 1, 2 and 3 between Anand Vihar and Faridabad. Route 1 has intermediate stops at Badarpur and Dilshad Garden. Route 2 has stops at Chanakyapuri and Dilshad Garden. The shortest route 3 with a length of 10 km stops at Chanakyapuri only, which is exactly at the middle of this route. The longest route has 3 km more length than the shortest one. The distance between Chanakyapuri and Dilshad Garden, Badarpur and Dilshad Garden, and Faridabad and Dilshad Garden are 4, 3 and 2 km, respectively.

Can you determine what is the distance between Anand Vihar and Badarpur?

27.

A computer program was tested 300 times before its release. The testing was done in three stages of 100 test each. If software failed 15 times in stage I, 12 times in stage II, 8 times in stage III, 6 times in stage I and stage II, 7 times in stage II and stage III. 4 times in stage I and stage III and 4 times in all the three stages.

Can you tell us how many times software failed in a single stage?

28.

Which letter replaces the question mark?

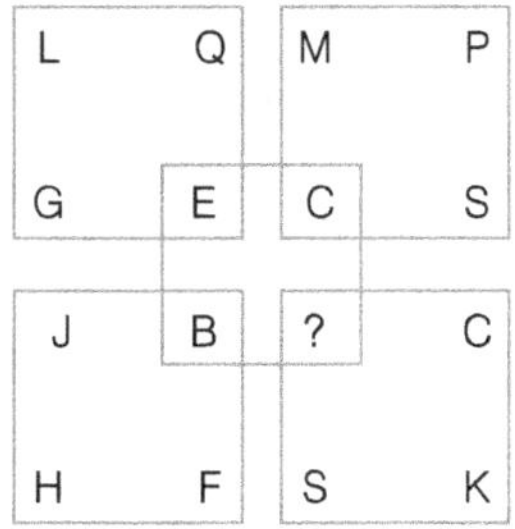

29.

Where does the missing hand go?

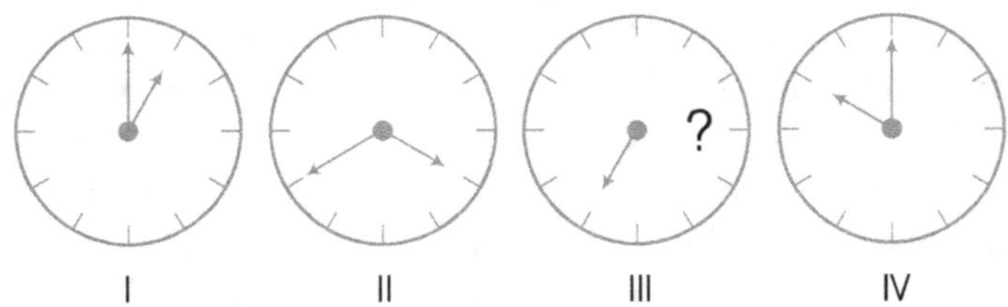

30.

Draw the correct pattern in the empty box to complete the pattern.

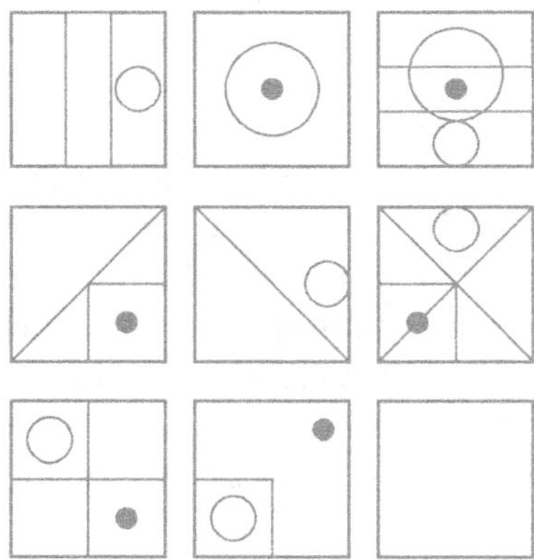

31.

Before sleeping Ken realised that he had to complete a novel to be discussed in his English class the next day. So, he decided to read that novel. When he started to read the novel, the lights went off and it was around 2 in the night. Ken lighted two uniform candles of equal length but one is thicker than other. The thick candle is supposed to last six hours and thin one three hours, when he finally went to sleep, the thick candle was twice as long as the thin one. Can you determine how long did Ken read in candle light?

32.

Mr. Petrick, the famous American architect was invited by MSM International Company on their new project launch to discuss with him the plan of constructing a new office building with a unique design. After a fortnight time Mr. Petrick suggested a design of a cubical building as shown in his model.

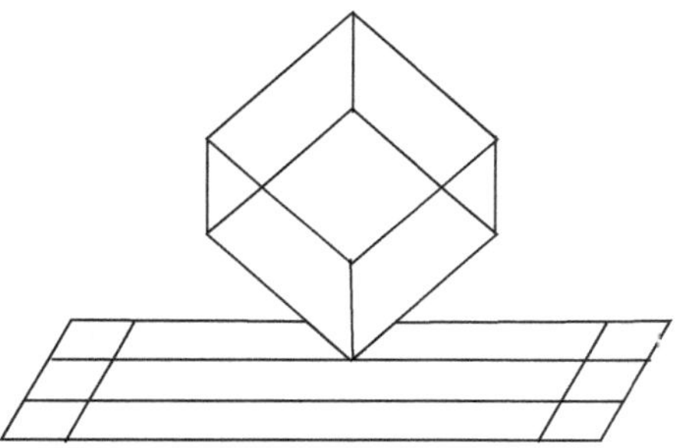

To keep the details as a secret Mr. Petrick wrote the design in the form of a puzzle, "Each outer surface of the building will be painted with the picture of six famous products of the company having different colours".

Wall surface with the picture of product 1 is opposite to the wall with picture of product 4 and wall with picture of product 2 is opposite to the picture of product 6. Wall surface with orange colour has picture of product 1. The wall surface having opposite face of orange coloured surface is black and has picture of product 4.

If you are facing wall with orange colour, then the top wall is pink coloured and has picture of product 3 on it. When the wall which is coloured grey is faced, then the picture of product 1 will be on top, product 2 picture on its right and blue coloured wall on its left. Also, white and blue coloured wall are on opposite faces. Mr. Petrick made his assistant read out the puzzle and asked him, if he could find out which four walls are adjacent to grey colour wall?

33.

Seven friends of mine have qualified in the preliminary round of Tata Crucible Business Quiz Contest. From these seven, two teams must be founded an orange team and a blue team, each team consisting of exactly three contestants. No contestant can be selected for more than one team. Based on performance of preliminary round, team selection is subject to the following restrictions.

Joginder cannot be in the same team as Kulvinder.

Ravinder cannot be in the same team as Sukhvinder.

If Arvinder is in the orange team, Ravinder if selected must be in the blue team.

If Mahinder is in the orange team, Kulvinder must be selected for the blue team.

If Mahinder is in the orange team, which two other persons should be selected in orange team?

34.

While allotting Spectrum TRAI (Telephone Regulatory Authority of India) divided 12 towns grouped into 4 zones with 3 towns per zone. It is intended to connect the towns with telephone lines such that every two towns are connected with three direct lines, if they belong to the same zone and with only one direct line otherwise. How many direct telephone lines are required?

Which of the bottom six grids completes this pattern?

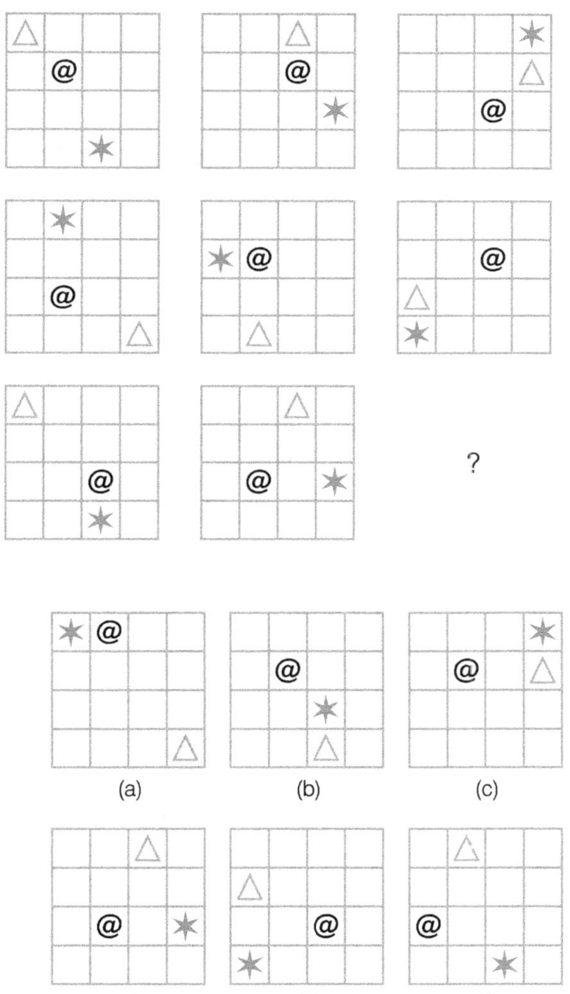

36.

With the increasing cases of mid way failure of Air India Airlines planes, a team of engineers was appointed to detect the major cause of it. The team of engineers divided themselves into small groups of five to scrunitize every intricate details.

Going by each machine the team realised that some machines are fitted by an irregular part. To fix the problem a team of technicians was sent to check the machines having that part and replace it.

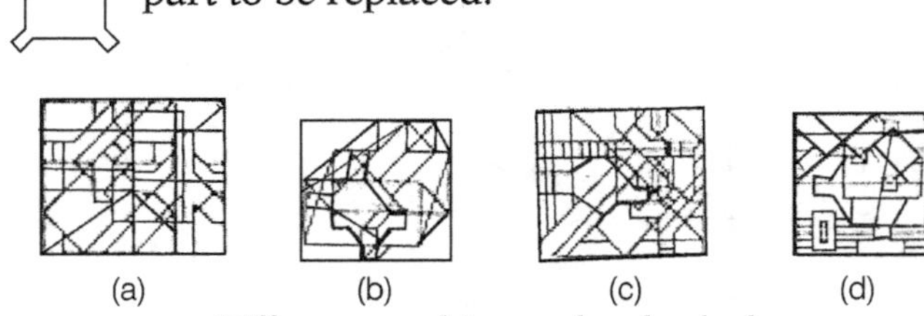

part to be replaced.

(a)   (b)   (c)   (d)

Different machines to be checked

Can you try to help the technicians find out which of the machine have that part implanted?

37.

Which letter goes in the empty segment to complete the sequence?

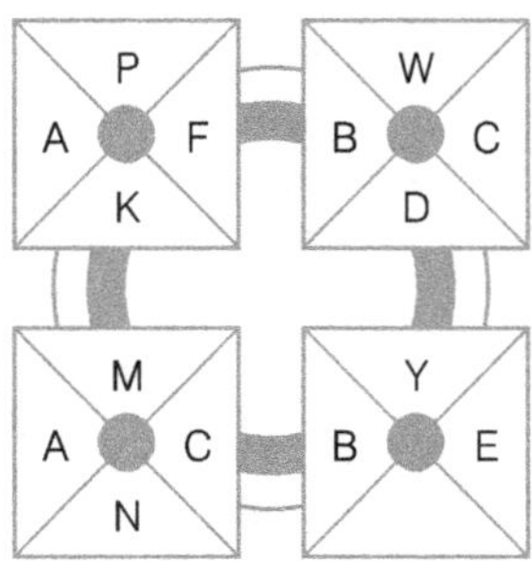

38.

The call centres of Delhi work in different batches and each batch is controlled through electronic mechanism, which generates passcode for 5 batches everyday, as follows:

Input

See the little squirrels jumping here and there.

Passcodes

Batch I   Jumping see here the and little there squirrels. (10 am to 11 am)

Batch II   The and here little see there jumping squirrels. (11 am to 12 noon)

Batch III   See the there and jumping here squirrels little. (12 noon to 1 pm)

Batch IV   Jumping there here the squirrels see little and. (1 pm to 2 pm)

Rest hour   ————————— (2 pm to 3 pm)

Batch V   The and squirrels jumping see there little here. (3 pm to 4 pm)

On a particular day, Mr Tarun Alex, the project head was to begin the work in the batch at 11 : 00 am. With a passcode 'he slowly records to his inner apartment intellect'. However, he came late on that day and hence joined the batch at 12 noon.

What was his passcode at that time?

Here's a third Venn diagram challenge devised by philosophy teacher Mr. Alexis as a warm-up for his students. He draws the diagram and writes his challenge on the whiteboard in the classroom.

Which areas of this diagram represent:

1. Black cats with white feet who like fish but don't have fleas?
2. Grey cats with white feet who have fleas but don't like fish?
3. Ginger cats without white feet who like fish and have fleas?
4. Cats with black fur and black feet who like fish but don't have fleas?
5. White-footed black cats who scratch at their fleas and gobble up fish?
6. Cats with black fur, white feet and fleas who refuse all foods except finely sliced cooked chicken?

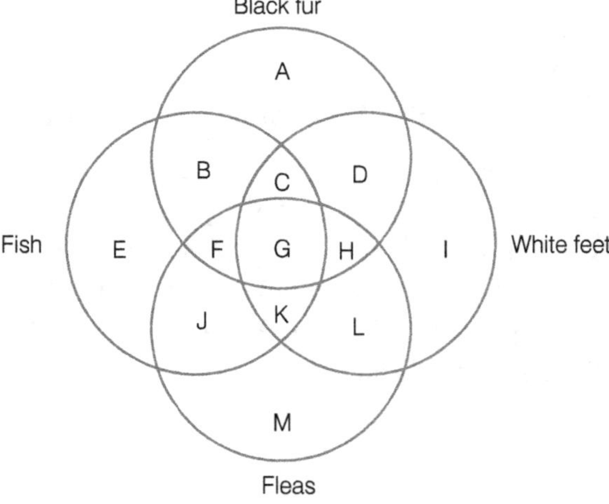

40.

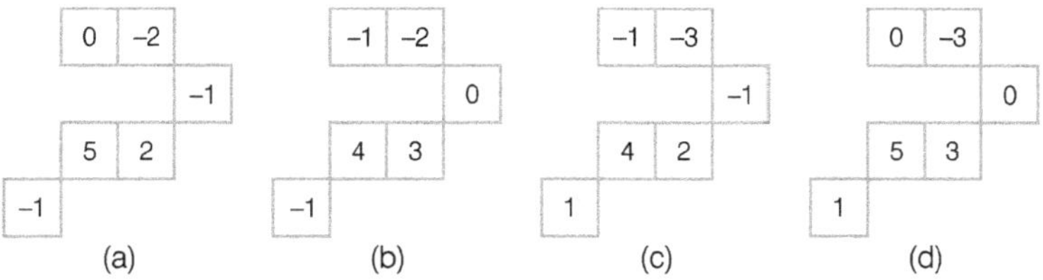

Which is the missing section?

(a)   (b)   (c)   (d)

41.

Three Goddesses were sitting in an old India Temple. Their names were truth (always telling the truth), lie (always lying) and wisdom (sometimes lying).

A visitor asked the one on the left. "Who is sitting next to you?"

'Truth', she answered.

Then, he asked the one in the middle, 'who are you?'

'Wisdom', she answered.

Lastly he asked the one on the right. Who is your neighbour?

'Lie', she answered.

Then, it became clear who is who.

Can you determine who is telling the truth?

42.

My uncle Khurana has two pets namely Aishwarya (a beautiful cat) and Brunu (a dangerous dog). When we reached his home, he told us that he is going to tell us the story of his pets but in the language of numbers and if you are able to understand what I meant by that number then I will believe that I have intelligent nephews. He said '816321' which means 'the brown dog frightened the cat, '64851' means 'the frightened cat ran away'. '7621' means 'the cat was brown' and '341' means 'the dog ran.' Then, he say now, tell me what will I say for 'the dog was frightened'?

43.

Walmart Retail Store has started seven branches in the city of Bengaluru namely W1, W2, W3, W4, W5, W6, W7 and central Distribution Centre (DC). The nearest branch to DC is W6, which is in the South of DC and is 9 km away from DC. W2 is 17 km away from DC in the West. The branch W1 is 11 km away from W2 further in the West. The branch W3 is 11 km in the North-East of W1. W4 is 13 km away from W3 in the East. W5 is 11 km in the North-East of the DC.

In the North-East of W6 is W7 and the distance between them is 15 km. The distance between W1 and W6, W2 and W6, W6 and W5 is 23 km, 19 km, 13 km, respectively. W3 is 14 km away from DC in the North-West direction, while W2 is also 14 km away from W4. A truck carrying some goods starts from the distribution centre and has to cover atleast four stores in single trip. There is an essential good that has to be delivered in the store W7, but the delivery at W7 has to be done in the end.

Can you determine what is the shortest distance the truck would travel?

44.

In 30th India International Trade Fair, there was unique system of managing the people and they were allowed in the different batches, so the ground inside the Pragati Maidan is manageable. The fair is open for the public, from 9 am to 3 pm and again, from 4 pm to 10 pm. In a day, there are 12 batches of 1 hour each. The entry ticket bears a passcode made of seven words, which changes every hour following a particular rule.

The passcodes for 4 pm to 10 pm are same as those for respective hours during 9 am to 3 pm, i.e. the passcode for 4 pm to 5 pm is same as that of 9 am to 10 am and so on. Following is an illustration of the code and steps of rearrangement for subsequent clock hours.

Batch I   9 am to 10 am (4 pm to 5 pm)
Passcode   dig more and you will find water.

Batch II   10 am to 11 am (5 pm to 6 pm)
Passcode   and dig find you water will more.

Batch III 11 am to 12 noon (6 pm to 7 pm)
Passcode   find and will you more water dig.
               and so on ....

Can you tell me if the passcode for the second batch is 'do not play the near water dirty', then what will be the passcode for 2 pm to 3 pm batch?

45.

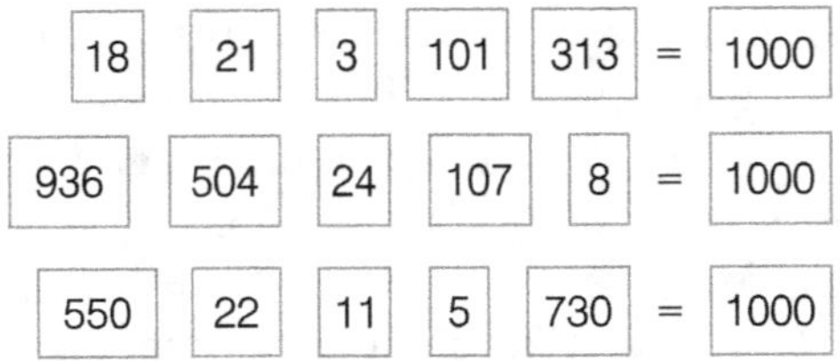

Here are three separate challenges. Your 1st task is to insert the four different mathematical operations (addition, subtraction, multiplication and division) between the boxes in each equation in such a way that the final outcome is one thousand. You must perform each mathematical operation in the order in which it appears.

46.

This riddle is (at least for me) very hard to imagine ...
You have an appliance like this:

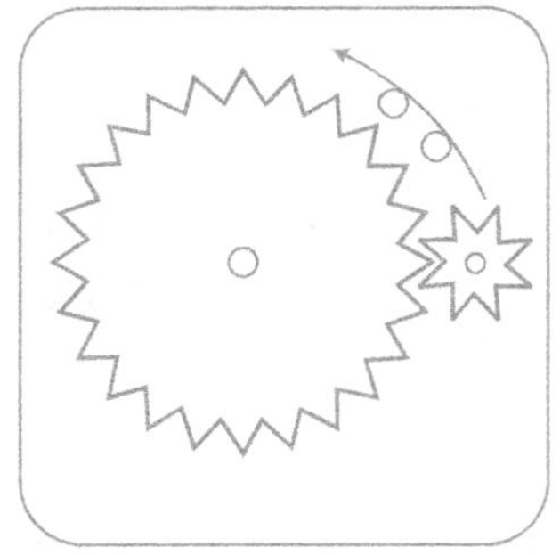

There are two cogwheels in a box. The bigger one has 24 teeth and it is tightly attached to the centre of the box (it doesn't turn or move). The smaller one has 8 teeth and it rotates around the bigger wheel. How many times does the smaller wheel turn compared with the box when it turns once around the bigger wheel?

47.

In a seminar, there was huge uproar for the crime against women. They were chanting two slogans regularly.

Slogan I Is there any respect for women is left in the world.

Slogan II All metros except small have failed to secure women.

A press reporter available in the seminar made few conclusions which were as follow:

Conclusion I Women life is at risk and hazard.

Conclusion II Molestation of women has increased in metropolitan cities.

Conclusion III Small towns are safer for women.

Conclusion IV Women should start living in small towns.

Can you determine which of these conclusions is/are valid conclusion(s) made by the reporter?

48.

Perry comes home on his birthday and finds that his brother has left four notes in the kitchen—one on the fridge, one on the cupboard door, one on the breadbox and one on the oven, plus a fifth on the front door that says: "Happy Birthday, Perry. Your present is in the kitchen. But only one of the notes you'll find there is truthful!"

The four notes in the kitchen read as follows:

The fridge note says: "Your birthday present's in the cupboard or the oven!"

The cupboard note says: "Your birthday present's in the fridge or the breadbox!"

The oven note says: "Your birthday present's here!"

The note on the breadbox says: "Your birthday present's not here!"

Help Perry to find out his birthday present.

49.

Mr Maan Singh is the world's oldest father, who resides in Rajasthan and have 8 children. He has 5 sons namely Arun, Mahi, Rohit, Nilesh and Sourav and 3 daughters namely Tamanna, Kuntala and Janaki. The 3 sons of Mr Maan Singh were born first followed by 2 daughters. Sourav is the eldest child and Janaki is the youngest. All his children are sponsored by Government of Rajasthan to study in Convent School. 3 of his children are studying at Trinity School and 3 are studying at St Stephen's School.

Tamanna and Rohit study at St Stephen School. Kuntala, the eldest daughter, plays chess. Mansarovar School offers cricket only, while Trinity School offers chess. Besides, these schools offer no other games. The children, who are at Mansarover School have been born in succession. Mahi and Nilesh are cricketers, while Arun plays football. Rohit, who was born just before Janaki, plays hockey.

Can you determine the position of Arun born as the child of Maan Singh and game is played by him and the school in which he studies?

50.

The given diagram shows the ring road in Delhi along with the several routes following these:

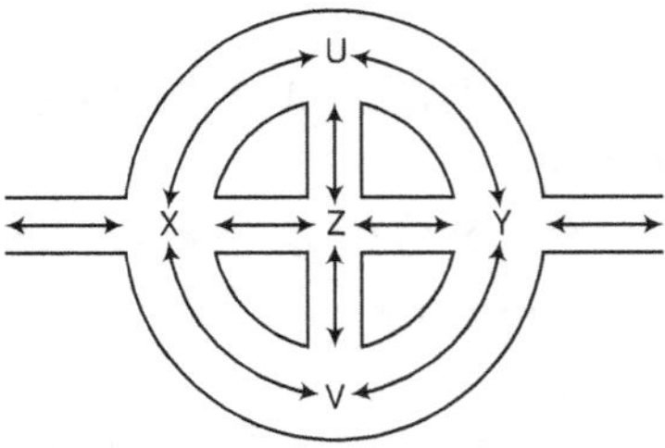

Can you determine the maximum number of bus routes possible from X to Y, so that the bus does not come to one junction more than once in a route?

51.

The entry ticket for the World Book Fair, 2015 at Pragati Maidan, New Delhi bears a password which is changed after every clock hour based on set of words chosen for everyday. The following is the illustration of the code and the steps of rearrangement for subsequent clock hours. The timing is 9 am to 3 pm.

Batch I (9 am to 10 am) is not ready cloth simple harmony burning.

Batch II (10 am to 11 am) ready not is cloth burning harmony simple.

Batch III (11 am to 12 noon) cloth is not ready simple harmony burning.

Batch IV (12 noon to 1 pm) not is cloth ready burning harmony simple.

Batch V (1 pm to 2 pm) ready cloth is not simple harmony burning
and so on.

If the day's first password is 'Camel road no toy say me not'.

What will be the password for IV batch i.e. 12 noon to 1 pm?

52.

The country like Spain has very intelligent mechanism for road safety and computers are given training to follow the road safety mechanism. For the purpose they have installed two boards indicating the several commands for the computers.

Board I

	0	1	2	3	4
0	F	O	M	S	R
1	S	R	F	O	M
2	O	M	S	R	F
3	R	F	O	M	S
4	M	S	R	F	O

Board II

	5	6	7	8	9
5	A	T	D	I	P
6	I	P	A	T	D
7	T	D	I	P	A
8	P	A	T	D	I
9	D	I	P	A	T

Can you tell what numbers will be indicated on two boards, common when there is signal for 'STOP' in Spain?

53.

In order to improve the sales of personal care products. Company gave instruction to all shopkeepers to promote six products (Ariel, Vivel, Rin, Nirma, Gillete gel and Pepsodent) which are to be placed in six display windows of a shop numbered 1-6 from left to right of a shopkeeper's standing outside the shop. As per the company requirement, Rin and Ariel should be displayed next to each other, but Ariel should be atleast three windows away from Nirma. Pepsodent is preferred to be kept between Gillete gel and Rin but away from Vivel atleast by two windows. Vivel cannot be displayed next to Rin for the reason of mixed product identity. Also, Vivel cannot be displayed in window 1.

Can you determine which of the above product is displayed left to Ariel?

54.

Rongali Bihu is a famous cultural festival in Assam. People over there celebrate it, as the harvesting season. On this occasion, a small farmer asks his daughter to make a rangoli, which is symbol of prosperity, but she was asked to use the minimum number of colours, which are not adjacent to each other.

Can you help the farmer's daughter in filling colours to rangoli?

55.

Two cyclists were consulting a road map in preparation for a little tour together. The circles represent towns and all the good roads are represented by lines. They are starting from the town with a star and must complete their tour at E. But before arriving there they want to visit every other town once and only once. That is the difficulty. Mr Spicer said, "I am certain we can find a way of doing it," but Mr Maggs replied, "No way, I'm sure." Now, which of them was correct? Take your pencil and see if you can find any way of doing it. Of course you must keep to the roads indicated.

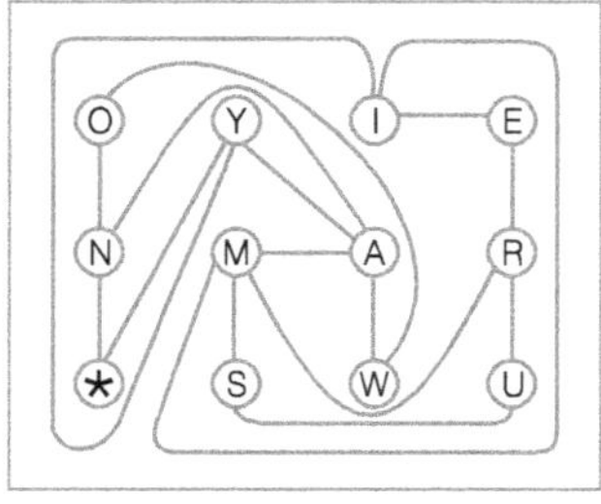

56.

While travelling in a train I met four people, each one of them belongs to different states namely Uttar Pradesh (UP), Madhya Pradesh (MP), Tamil Nadu (TN) and Andhra Pradesh (AP), when I asked them about the state to which they belonged, each one of them made two statements. Atleast one person among them is a truth teller (who always speaks the truth). Atleast one person among them is a liar (who always lies). Atleast one of them is an alternator (who alternates between the truth and lie in any order). The replies were as follow:

Puneet I am from Andhra Pradesh, Velu is from Uttar Pradesh.

Velu Navin is from Madhya Pradesh, Rajni is from Andhra Pradesh.

Navin I am from Tamil Nadu, Puneet is from Tamil Nadu.

Rajni I am from Madhya Pradesh, Velu is from MP.

It is also known that Puneet is from Tamil Nadu.

Can you tell me the two people who made same number of true statements?

57.

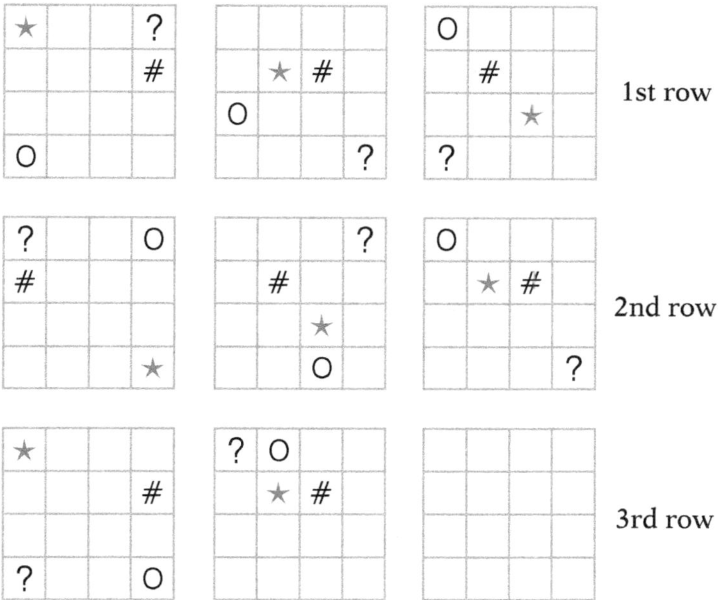

1st row

2nd row

3rd row

Which of the following options will correctly fill the third figure in third row?

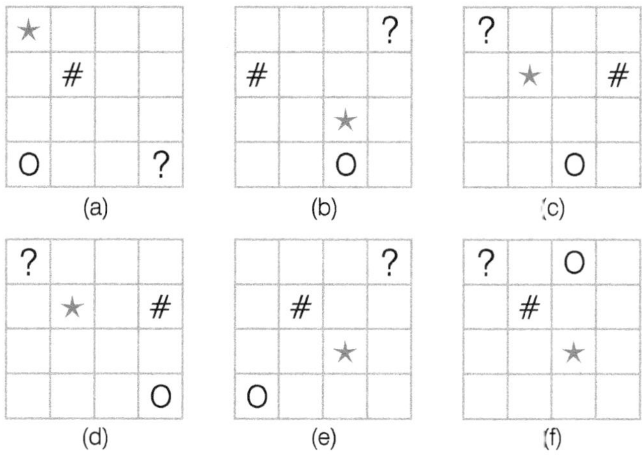

(a)   (b)   (c)

(d)   (e)   (f)

58.

Local sports clubs take turns to plant a tree each year in the town's main street. A bird has established a nest in each tree.

1. The crow lives in the beech tree.

2. The lime was planted two years after the tree planted by the golf club.

3. The robin is in the tree planted by the bowling club, which is next to the tree planted by the soccer club.

4. Jim planted his tree in 1971.

5. The starling is in the poplar tree planted by Desmond in 1974.

6. The robin lives in the tree planted by the bowling club, which is next to the tree planted by the soccer club.

7. Tony planted the middle tree—a beech.

8. Bill has an owl in his tree, which is next to the ash.

9. The tree at the right hand end was planted in 1974 by the soccer club.

10. The elm was planted in 1970.

11. The tennis club planted a tree in 1972.

12. The squash club planted a tree in 1970.

13. Sylvester planted his tree in 1973 and it has a robin in it.

14. The blackbird is in the tree planted by Jim.

Tree					
Person					
Club					
Bird					
Year					

Work out which tree was planted by which member of each club and in which year?

59.

Indian Army General, in order to save his crucial information intact decided to generate different codes to pass that information. With the help of his colleague, the General planned to send the codes in the form of impressions formed by folding papers. He carried a code protocol to check the applicability of the idea. For this purpose, he made a code by folding and cutting a piece of paper as shown below and asked his juniors to crack it and get into action.

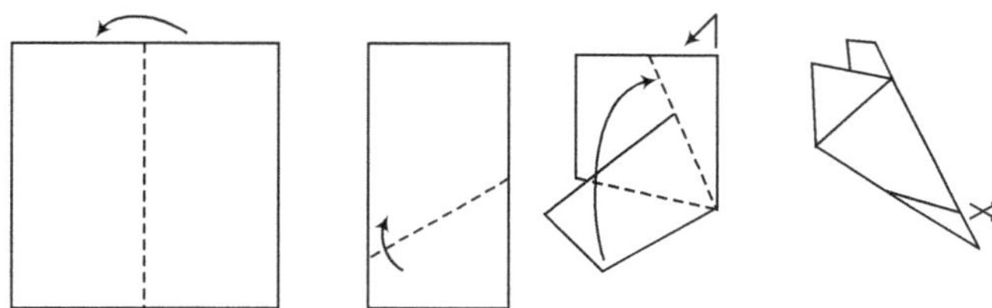

Following the above instructions, can you try to help the juniors crack the code by finding what shape would be formed?

60.

The city of Königsberg had seven bridges that crossed the river Pregel.

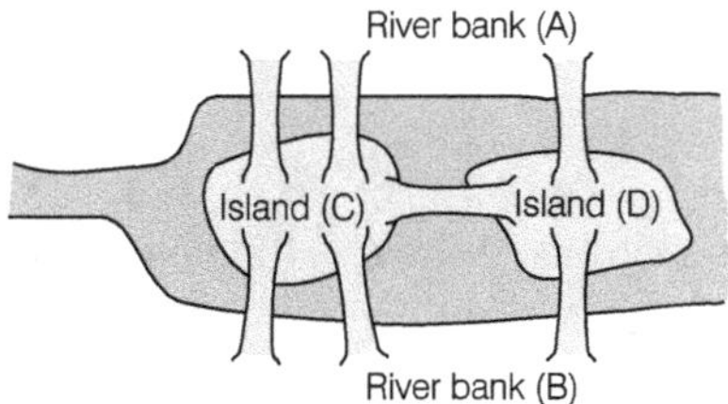

Can you find a way of crossing all the bridges exactly once?

You can't go over a bridge more than once.

61.

Michael and Matthew chipped in to buy a grinding wheel (22 inch in diameter) with a $3\frac{1}{7}$ inch mounting hole in the middle. Since, they live 10 miles apart, they agreed that Matthew would be the first to take it and when half of it would be used up, he would give it to Michael. What diameter will the wheel have when it changes hands?

Clue the circle's area is expressed in πR^2, where R is the length of the radius.

62.

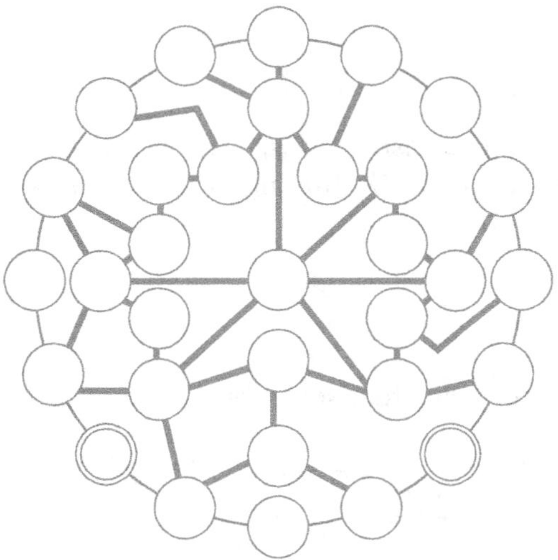

Here is a puzzle that offers two ways to solve. Your challenge is to trace two paths that contain an 'even' number of total rings beginning and ending at the double rings. Your first path must be the shortest possible route and your second path must be the longest possible route. No ring or connector may be used more than once per solution.

63.

During his five year studies, a student passed 33 exams. Each following year, he wrote fewer exams than the previous year. The number of his first year exams was three times greater than the number of his final year exams. How many exams did the student have in his third year?

64.

	Squirrel	Tree	Nuts
1.	Gerald	Birch	11
2.	Scamper	Sycamore	12
3.	Basil	Ash	10
4.	Tufty	Oak	9

Mr Prodder, the park keeper had spent the last few weeks observing squirrels. In fact, he had been so absorbed in watching them bury their nuts he had kept a record. The table he had made up showed the name he had assigned to the squirrel, the tree it lived in and the number of nuts he had seen it bury, logged in order according to the bushiness of their tails. The trouble was, he had misplaced his diary and had tried to reproduce the table from memory. Although he had recalled the entries correctly, he only managed to get one entry in each column correctly positioned. The correct table had the following properties:

(1) The squirrel that lived in the sycamore tree was one place below the one that had buried 12 nuts.

(2) The squirrel that had buried 10 nuts was one place above Tufty.

(3) The ash tree inhabitant was two places below Scamper.

(4) Second place did not belong to the squirrel that had buried 10 nuts.

Can you give the name, tree and number of nuts hidden for each position?

65.

For the intelligence bureau interview procedure the team of interviewers set some extra questions to ask the interviewee and judge their logical thinking skills. Siddhant, one of the interviewers, when went for his turn was asked one such question that if he was an officer and was given a task to search for a criminal who was hiding in one of the five rooms of a hotel and one of his colleague officers left out some hints in front of each room to catch the criminal which are as follow:

Room-1, Hint-1: The criminal is not in Room 2.

Room-2, Hint-2: The criminal is not in this room.

Room-3, Hint-3: The criminal is not in room 1.

Room-4, Hint-4: At least one of these five hints is false.

Room-5, Hint-5: Either this hint is false or the hint on the room with the criminal is true.

On the basis of it, Siddhant was asked to find in which room was the criminal hiding. Can you help Siddhant solving the puzzle?

66.

Indian Oil Corporation has different batches of employees involved in oil extraction. The different batches are controlled by electronic mechanism, which generates pass codes for the 6 batches each day as follow:

Input These icons were taken out from the sea.

Batch I From sea the out taken were icons these.

Batch II From icons these were taken out the sea.

Batch III From icons out sea the taken were these.

Batch IV From icons out sea these were taken the and so on.

The first batch starts at 10:00 am and each batch is for one hour. There is rest period of one hour after the end of the IV batch.

Can you tell us, if the code for the batch at 1:00 pm on a day was "back go here people, who settle want to", what was the passcode for the batch at 3:00 pm on that day?

67.

A Venn diagram is a way of communicating relationships. For example, the following Venn diagrams show that

(1) all beetles and all flies are insects and

(2) some mammals and some insects can fly.

Using this type of visual scheme, sketch out Venn diagrams that illustrate the following:

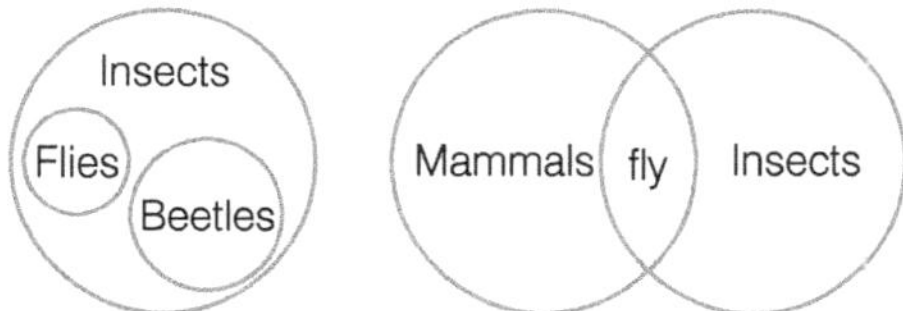

1. All ice creams are dairy products and all dairy products are food.

2. Some rockets use liquid fuel, some rockets use solid fuel and the space shuttle uses both liquid and solid fuel.

3. All whales and all dogs have hair. All snakes do not have hair.

68.

Each letter of the alphabet has been given a different value from 1 to 26. Next to the list of words are the total values of the letters contained in each word. What is the value of each letter of the alphabet?

BEG = 59, CALL = 48, CHIEF = 36, CRAZY = 60, DEN = 53,

GAME = 47, GUN = 51, HAM = 16, HAVE = 40, IF = 11,

JACK = 24, KEY = 43, LAZE = 57, MAP = 28, MOVE = 58,

NEON = 86, OXEN = 82, PALM = 47, QUIT = 40,

QUITE = 60, STALL = 80, TALK = 39,

TORE = 73, VAST = 51, WALK = 54

If $T = 11$, $C = 2$, $H = C + 1$ and $F = T - 7$, then what is the total value of the word 'WEBSITE'?

69.

Five wineglasses have been arranged in a row as shown in the picture below and numbered from 1 to 5.

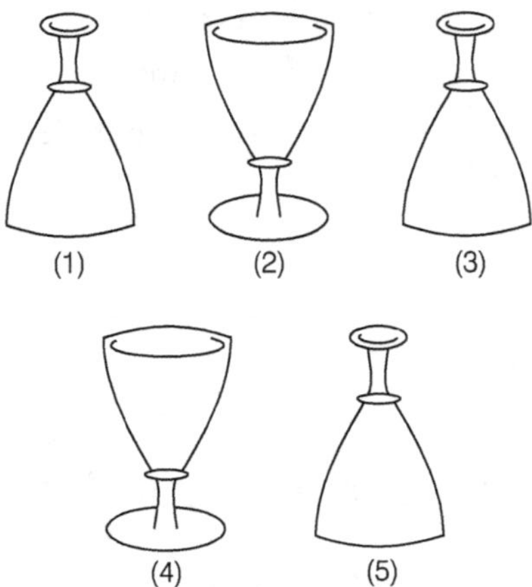

Two players take part in the game and they make moves in turns. However, only two kinds of moves are allowed:

1. Any wineglass standing stem side up can be placed the other way round, i.e. stem side down.

2. You can turn two wineglasses standing side by side if the one standing on the right is upside down.

The winner is the player after whose move all the glasses will be standing on their stems. Does the player beginning the game have a winning strategy (i.e. he can always win, irrespective of what his opponent does)?

70.

At this school the boys sit at desks numbered 1-5 and the girls sit opposite them at desks numbered 6-10.

1. The girl sitting next to the girl opposite desk number 1 is Fiona.
2. Fiona is three desks away from Grace.
3. Hilary is opposite to Colin.
4. Eddy is opposite the girl next to Hilary.
5. If Colin is not central than Alan is.
6. David is next to Bill.
7. Bill is three desks away from Colin.
8. If Fiona is not central than Indira is.
9. Hilary is three desks away from Jane.
10. David is opposite to Grace.
11. The girl sitting next to the girl opposite Alan is Jane.
12. Colin is not at desk number 5.
13. Jane is not at desk number 10.

Can you work out the seating arrangements?

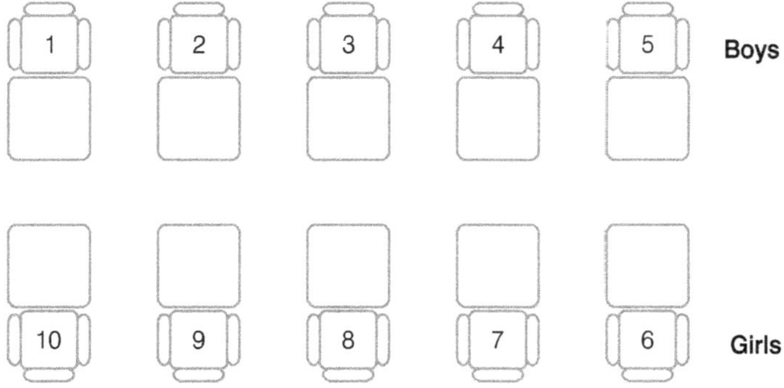

39

71.

6	2	5	1
3	1	4	7
4	1	9	5
3	1	2	4

In this game, there are two players. The 1st player can split the matrix vertically into 2 equal halves and choose one half for further play. The next move on this half is by the other player who will split it horizontally and choose one half for further play. The game will continue in this manner. At the end the last number left is the first player gain.

If you start the game, retain the right half and again right half after your opponent move.

Can you determine how should your opponent play to minimise your gain if he has four chances (a) retain upper, retain lower (b) retain upper, retain upper (c) retain lower, retain upper (d) retain lower, retain lower.

72.

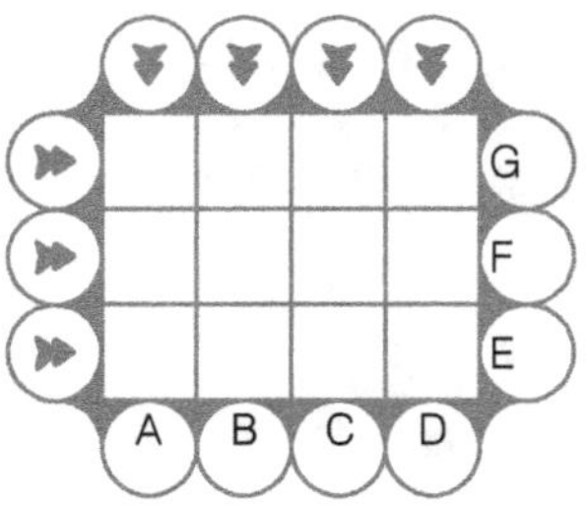

Beginning at the letter 'A', position a series of seven consecutive numbers from lowest to highest in the seven circles. Next, select another series of twelve consecutive numbers and place them in the twelve squares so that the sum of each horizontal and vertical row will total the number in the respective circle.

73.

At the cake shop, there are three types of cakes – their prices are in round dollars. For a dollar, you can get a cream cake, two fruit cakes, or three doughnuts. Two brothers, Jeremy and Roger, had been given $11 by their parents and invited a group of backyard kids to have cakes together. The group consisted of as many boys and girls. Each kid was treated to the same set of cakes, which consisted of the same number of the same cakes. How big was the group of kids?

74.

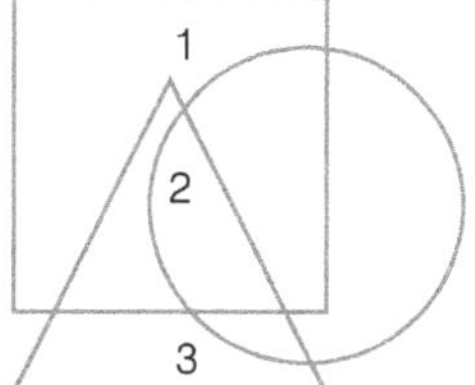

Place the remaining numbers from one to ten in the seven divisions of this overlapping geometric configuration to fulfil the following requirements:

1. The circle, square and triangle must individually total thirty.

2. The three outer divisions of the circle, square and triangle must also total thirty.

75.

During a school trip attended by all Class 5B pupils, there arose several misunderstandings, which resulted in the class dividing into two separate groups. If Sophie decided to leave group 1 and join group 2, the first one would number 1/3 of the class. If, however, Adam, Michael and Will left the second group for the first, the latter would make up half of the class. How many pupils attend Class 5B?

76.

During a country ramble Mr and Mrs Softleigh found themselves in a pretty little dilemma. They had to cross a stream in a small boat which was capable of carrying only 150 lbs weight. But Mr Softleigh and his wife each weighed exactly 150 lbs, and each of their sons weighed 75 lbs. And then there was the dog, who could not be induced on any terms to swim.

On the principle of 'ladies first', they at once sent Mrs Softleigh over, but this was a stupid oversight, because she had to come back again with the boat, so nothing was gained by that operation. How did they all succeed in getting across?

77.

A survey was conducted by Viacom International among 200 mobile users of different companies. It was found that 160 users use mobile phones of Nokia, 100 use mobile phones of Samsung and 90 use mobile phones of Apple. 20 use the mobile phones of all the three companies and each one uses mobile phone of atleast one of the three companies. Can you tell us, how many use mobile phones of only one company?

78.

A certain rabbit keeper brought his rabbits to the market. The first customer bought 1/6 of all the animals +1; the second buyer again took 1/6 of the remaining rabbits + 2; the third customer bought 1/6 of the remaining animals + 3 and so on. When the man had sold all his rabbits, he found to his surprise that each customer had bought the same number of rabbits. How many rabbits did the salesman bring to the market and how many customers did he have?

79.

Del operates a delivery service, taking small consignments from one town to another for private customers and small businesses. Last week, he made five journeys. Can you discover not only from where and to where he travelled, but also his load on each day? The following clues contain all the information you'll need.

1. Del delivered several boxes of fruit for a small company the day before he went to Foursham, but later in the week than his journey from Eastering.

2. The cheese was transported earlier in the week than the shoes, which weren't collected in Northbrook.

3. Monday's trip wasn't to Threeton and Saturday's wasn't from Southford.

4. One journey was from Westbury to Oneford and this took place either the day before or the day after the job that involved taking a consignment of stationery to Firewood.

5. The trip to Twobury (not from Northbrook) took place two days later than that which started from Middleham.

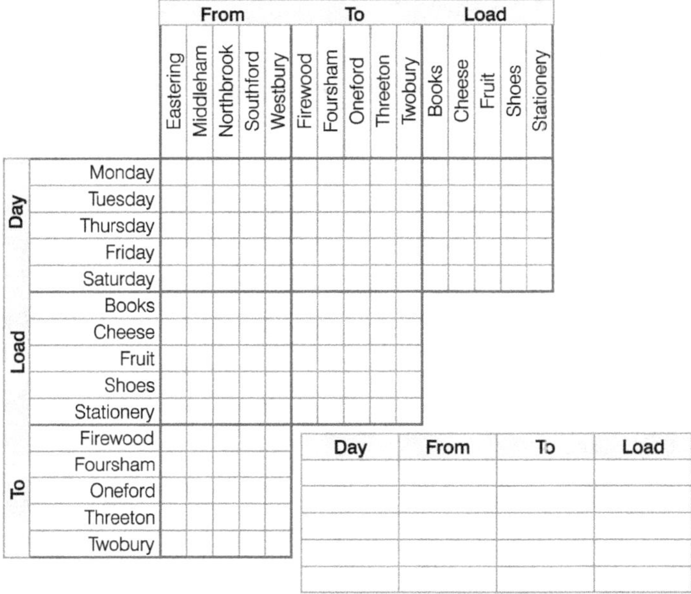

80.

	Pet	Street 1	Street 2
1.	Cat	Grunter	Road
2.	Dog	Hollow	Drive
3.	Elephant	Rubble	Crescent
4.	Alligator	Tempest	Avenue
5.	Parakeet	Apple	Walk
6.	Frog	Purple	Lane

Turtle Town was holding its annual Prize Pets competition and the first six places had already been decided. The pets were listed along with the street they came from, each street having a two-part name. However, the order presented to the master of ceremonies was not that decided on by the judges. The competition secretary had drunk one beer too many and although he managed to get each item in the correct column, only one item in each column was correctly positioned. The following facts were certain about the correct order.

1. Rubble was two places above the alligator and three places above Drive.

2. Neither Purple nor Tempest were fifth.

3. Avenue was one place below the dog and one place above Purple.

4. Fifth place was occupied by neither Avenue nor Lane.

5. Neither the parakeet nor the cat were second.

6. Crescent was one place below Hollow and three places above the frog.

Can you give the pet name and both parts of the street name for each position?

81.

Three college students – Anne, Bess and Candice – each studies four subjects. Two of them study Physics; two study Algebra; two study English; two study History; two study French; two study Japanese.

Anne   if she studies Algebra then she also takes History;

if she studies History she does not take English;

if she studies English she does not take Japanese.

Candice if she studies French she does not take Algebra;

if she does not study Algebra she studies Japanese;

if she studies Japanese she does not take English.

Bess   if she studies English she also takes Japanese;

if she studies Japanese she does not take Algebra;

if she studies Algebra she does not take French.

What do you know about these three students?

	Anne	Bess	Candice
Physics			
Algebra			
English			
History			
French			
Japanese			

82.

	Animal	Name	Prize
1.	Badger	Karen	Porsche
2.	Elephant	Harry	Spoon
3.	Antelope	Lorena	Television
4.	Cat	Ian	Microwave
5.	Dog	George	Carrot
6.	Frog	Jenny	Radiator

At Booliba Village, the animals had decided to have a race between two sticks set 100 m apart. The first six places were written down with the animal, its name and the prize for that position. Unfortunately, although each item was in the correct column, only one item in each column was correctly positioned. The following facts are true about the correct positions:

(1) Neither Badger nor George are sixth.

(2) Microwave is two places below Harry and one above elephant.

(3) Ian did not get carrot and is not next to Lorena.

(4) Spoon is three places below Ian and two below dog.

(5) Porsche is one place below Lorena and one above antelope.

Can you find the correct animal, name and prize for each position?

83.

Child spy Harry Starrs is whiling away time on a stakeout and devises this version of the game "Patience" for his partner Hank. He draws twelve cards A-L, as shown and asks Hank, "What is the face value and suit of each of the cards?"

Here are Harry's ground rules. Together the cards total 84. All twelve cards are of different values. (In the pack, the value of each card is as per its number, while Ace = 1, Jack = 11, Queen = 12 and King = 13) No card is horizontally or vertically next to another of the same colour and there are four different suits in each horizontal row and three different suits in each vertical column. In addition:

1. The 6 is next to and above the 10, which is next to and above the 2 of Spades.

2. Card C has a value three lower than that of card F, which has a value three lower than that of card L, which has a higher value than that of card A.

3. The Ace of Hearts is next to and above a card with a value three higher than that of card H, which is of the same suit as card C.

4. The Jack of Diamonds is in the same horizontal row as a Club with a value two higher than that of card B.

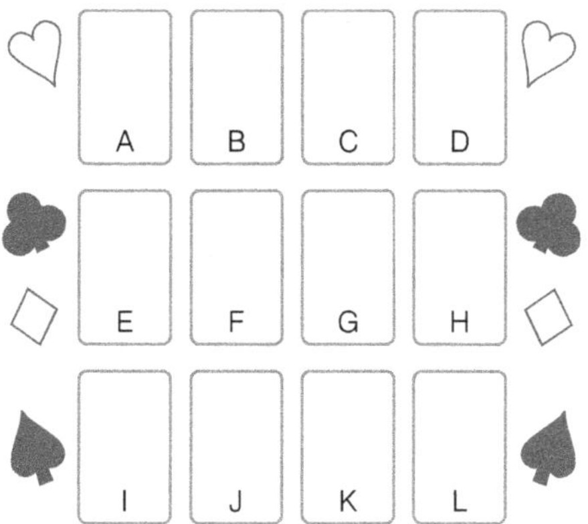

84.

You have just arrived to Wild West and you have already got in trouble. Buffalo Bill and Killer Kid are aiming at each other with colts. They accept you to death match with pleasure. They don't want to waste bullets so they agree on following rules:

1. Participants shoot in given order until only one survives.

2. Everyone shoots only once when it's his turn.

3. If someone is injured the others finish him off with iron rod.

4. The worst shooter (you) shoots first the best shoots last.

What tactics will you choose if you know that you hit about every third shot, Bill has around 50% chance and Immortal Kid never miss? (Please don't shoot yourself)

85.

The chief of Navy got an information of a ship sailing in ocean with illegal goods. He then ordered the captain of the ship to move in search of that ship in the ocean. While covering some distance the chief spotted the ship loaded with illegal goods sailing 7 km away from his ship on a way aligned in East-West direction. The chief is sailing on the Eastern side while the other ship is on the Western side of the island. On spotting the chief, the smuggler tries to speed up by sailing away with a uniform speed of $9\sqrt{2}$ km/h in a direction making an angle of 45° with island towards North-East. The chief starts with his ship at the same instance to move with a uniform velocity of 15 km/h and catches the ship of illegal goods.

Can you determine the time taken by the chief to catch the ship?

86.

There are six friends, who retired from Central Secretariat and has decided to live in a miniature village of six buildings. The six buildings of different colours red, yellow, white, blue, green and orange are in a row. Each of these buildings belongs to a different person among Mr Dubey, Mr Sharma, Mr Roy, Mr Sanyal, Mr Tiwari and Mr Reddy.

The green building is three places to the right of Mr Dubey's building. Red building is three places to the right of Mr Sharma's building. White building is three places to the right of Mr Reddy's building. Roy's building is adjacent to the orange building. Mr Sanyal's building is not green. Mr Sharma's building is not blue. Mr Tiwari's building is not adjacent to Roy's building but three places away from Mr Reddy's building.

Can you determine to whom the red building belonged to?

87.

World Athletic Meet 2013 was conducted in London. There were many athletes who participated but only four athletes namely Johnson, Bolt, Lewis and Powell completed in each of the four different events 100 m, 200 m, 400 m and 800 m race. These athletes finished in top four positions and no athlete finished any two events in the same position. The athlete who finished first in 100 m finished fourth in 800 m. The athlete who finished second in 200 m finished last in 100 m and Lewis is not the last one to finish 200 m. Johnson finished after Bolt in 200 m and 800 m.

Can you determine who is the first to finish 400 m race?

88.

There was a meeting of the chancellors of the university who were having talks regarding the teachers. They made the following statements followed by conclusions and several possibilities.

Can you check out the validity of several possibilities to find the valid possibility on the following grounds?

Statement I   Teachers are frequently professors.

Statement II   All lecturers except a few are teachers.

Conclusion I   Some teachers as well as some professors being lecturer is a possibility.

Conclusion II   All those teachers who are lecturers are also professors.

Possibility I   Only conclusion I is valid.

Possibility II   Only conclusion II is valid.

Possibility III   Both conclusions I and II are valid.

Possibility IV   Neither conclusion I nor II is valid.

89.

My bag can carry not more than 10 books. I must carry atleast one book each of management, mathematics, physics and fiction. Also, for every management book, I must carry two or more fictions and for every mathematics book, I must carry two or more physics books. I earn 4, 3, 2 and 1 points for each management, mathematics, physics and fiction book, respectively that I can carry in my bag. I want to maximise the points by carrying the most appropriate combination of books in my bag.

Can you determine what is the maximum point that I can earn?

90.

At Tihar Jail, Delhi, warden Samsher Singh Thapa was drunked one night and created a great nuisance. His jail consists of 100 cells in a line, all starting out closed. That night he gets drunk and goes along opening every single cell. He, then returns to the beginning and locked every second cell. He, then runs to the beginning again and locked every third cell, where if he encounters a cell in the sequence which is locked, he unlocks it and if it is unlocked, then he locks it (i.e. if while following the sequence (3, 6, 9, ...) if 6 is locked before then he will unlock it) then again with fourth cell and so on until the very last run in which he locked the hundredth cell and fells down from exhausion.

Can you tell us how many cells were left open after this process?

91.

A bag contains 7 green balls and 3 red ones. What is the probability of randomly taking out 3 green balls in succession without looking if:

A. Each ball is replaced before the next draw?

B. The balls are not replaced?

92.

Ten 6th grade pupils submitted 35 interesting math problems of their own. Among the participants, there was at least one person who submitted one problem, at least one that submitted two and at least one that submitted three. The most entries have been submitted by Steve. What is the smallest possible number of problems he could have submitted?

93.

Place the letters A, B, C, D, E, F, G, H and I into the grid of 9 squares using the following information:

I is in the same column as E which is not in the centre column. D is in the row below the row which contains F. A is in the row below the row which contains B. B is not in the first column. E is in the same row as F. C is in one of the four corner squares. G is in the square above A. F is in the same row as A and in the same column as C. E is in the row below the row which contains B. H is in the same row as I, the same column as F and is in a corner square.

94.

1	4	–3	–1	?
–3	?	?	–5	?
5	?	1	?	?
?	?	–5	–3	16
14	17	?	?	?

Which is the missing section?

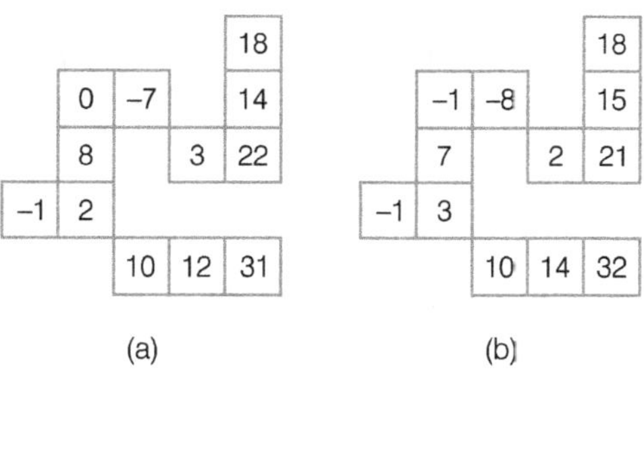

(a)   (b)

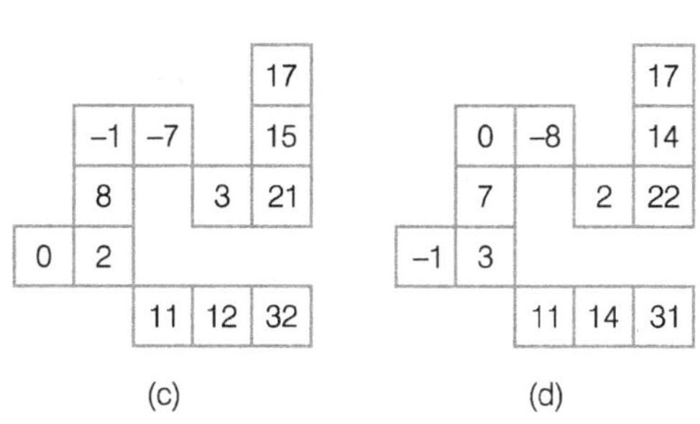

(c)   (d)

95.

Excitement grew as the crowd waited for the boxing match to commence. Fred 'the Needle'—so called because of his ferocious jab—glared across the ring at his opponent Brutal Ben. Everyone thought it was an even match; however, the contest lasted only eight consecutive punches, four from each man, the last punch knocking the other man out cold.

1. Fred's left jab was three punches after Ben's left uppercut.
2. Ben threw his right jab two punches before Fred delivered a right hook.
3. At one point during the exchange it was Fred, Fred again, then Ben, then Fred.
4. Fred's right uppercut was three punches before Ben's left hook.
5. Ben's right to the body was sometime after Fred's left to the body.

In what order were the eight punches thrown and who won?

96.

You've just thrown your first two dice in a craps game and your point is 10. This means that you must continue to roll the dice until you roll another 10 to make your point. If you roll a 7 before you roll another 10, you lose.

What are your chances of winning with 10 as your point?

97.

In my neighbourhood, there lived three naughty boys namely Imran, Rizwan and Kamran. One day they stole a basket full of apples from a nearby garden and hid the loot and went to sleep before retiring they did some quick counting and found that apples were less than a hundred in numbers.

During the night one boy woke up counted the apples and found that he could divide the apples in three equal parts if he first took one for himself. He then took one apple, ate it up and took 1/3 of the rest, hid them separately and went back to sleep shortly, thereafter another boy woke up counted the apple and he again found that he took one for himself and loot can be divided into three equal parts. He ate up one apple bugged 1/3 of the remainder hid them separately and went back to sleep.

The third boy also woke after sometime, did the same and went back to sleep. In the morning when all wake up and counted apples, they found that the remaining apples again totalled 1 more than could be divided into three equal parts. How many apples did the boy steal?

98.

The cells in this grid contain the digits 1 to 9 in random order.

Column A contains no odd digits.

Cell C_3 minus C_2 equals to 4.

The sum of three digits in row 1 is 17.

Number 7 is in column B, its left hand neighbours is not 4. The digit in column C add upto 14. 2 is not in the same horizontal row as 8 and 9 is not immediately below 3. Which cell holds the number 9?

	A	B	C
1			
2			
3			

99.

There are four animals. Each eats breakfast on the farm every morning. The following facts apply.

1. The horse eats in the shed or the house.
2. The animal that eats cornflakes is the horse or the cow but does not eat in the field.
3. The animal that eats in the barn has neither the toast nor the grits.
4. The goat does not eat the grits.
5. The animal that eats in the shed is the horse or the goat but does not eat toast.
6. The animal that eats the grits is not the cow and does not eat in the house.
7. The pig does not eat in the field and is not the porridge eater.
8. The cow does not eat in the house.

Can you match each animal with a breakfast and location?

100.

Thirteen different years are listed next to the grid below. Using the digits totals next to each column and row, fit the 13 yr into the grid, vertically or horizontally. Some of the years overlap and each column and row contains at least one year. Two digits and one year have been entered for you as a start.

1121						9	27	1433
1189						1	17	1452
1194		4				4	19	1468
1232						3	26	1711
1272						3	13	1873
1426	6	19	16	21	20	20		1921
								1941

101.

A jailer has a large number of prisoners to guard and has to seat them at a number of tables at mealtimes. The regulations state the following seating arrangements:

1. Each table is to seat the same number of prisoners.

2. The number at each table is to be an odd number.

The jailer finds that when he seats the prisoners:

> 3 per table, he has 2 prisoners left over;
>
> 5 per table, he has 4 prisoners left over;
>
> 7 per table, he has 6 prisoners left over;
>
> 9 per table, he has 8 prisoners left over;

but when he seats them 11 per table there are none left over.

How many prisoners are there?

102.

Blind Pugh was after hidden treasure, just like the rest of his shipmates, but could not see the map of Treasure Island. However, his hearing was shipshape, and he intended to locate the treasure from what he overheard and get there before the others. The island was divided into a 4×4 grid of equal squares, each square having a unique colour. He had heard the following facts:

1. The blue square was one square horizontally to the left of the pink square.
2. The orange was one to the right of and one above the white.
3. The red was one square vertically above the purple.
4. The lavender was one square horizontally to the left of the indigo.
5. The brown was one vertically below the green.
6. The purple was one horizontally to the left of the grey.
7. The violet was two horizontally to the right of the yellow.
8. The indigo was one vertically above the white.
9. The turquoise was two below and one to the right of the red.
10. The crimson was one to the right of and one below the green.
11. The gold square indicates where the gold is buried.
    Where was the gold?

103.

The palm spring voice is an International singing competition where only married couples are allowed to participate. Four married couples competed in this competition. Each couple had a unique team name. The points scored by the teams were 2, 4, 6 and 8. The 'Sweet couple' won 2 points. The 'Bindas singers' won two more points than Laxman's team, Mukesh's team won four points more than Leena's team, but Leena's team didn't score the least amount of points. 'Just singing' won 6 points. Waheda was not on the team called 'New singers'. Sanjeev's team won 4 points. Divya was not on the 'Bindas singers' team. Tapas and Sania were on the same team but it was not the 'Sweet couple'.

Can you determine who was Laxman's teammate and the teams name?

104.

Five student friends are at university, reading different subjects. They see one another regularly as they all cycle to their various lectures and always ping "Hello!" on their bicycle bells. Study the clues below to determine where each one has his or her lodgings, the subject he or she is taking at university, and the colour of his or her bicycle.

Clues

1. The student of History (not Hannah) lives in Saddle Street and has neither the silver nor the green bicycle.

2. Derek, who rides a startlingly bright orange bicycle, isn't studying History or Computing.

3. The student with lodgings in Wheel Way is neither Jimmy (who is studying Engineering) nor the student of Psychology (whose bicycle is neither green nor red).

4. The student with the silver bicycle is neither the one who lives in Handlebar Hill (who is studying Computing) nor Sharon, who lives in Chain Close.

		Lodgings					Studying					Bicycle				
		Bell Boulevard	Chain Close	Handlebar Hill	Saddle Street	Wheel Way	Computing	Engineering	History	Languages	Psychology	Green	Orange	Purple	Red	Silver
Student	Derek															
Student	George															
Student	Hannah															
Student	Jimmy															
Student	Sharon															
Bicycle	Green															
Bicycle	Orange															
Bicycle	Purple															
Bicycle	Red															
Bicycle	Silver															
Studying	Computing															
Studying	Engineering															
Studying	History															
Studying	Languages															
Studying	Psychology															

Student	Lodgings	Studying	Bicycle

105.

A Cockney friend, who is very apt to draw the long bow and is evidently less of a sportsman than he pretends to be, relates to me the following not very credible yarn:

"I've just been pheasant shooting with my friend the duke. We had splendid sport, and I made some wonderful shots. What do you think of this, for instance? Perhaps you can twist it into a puzzle. The duke and I were crossing a field when suddenly twenty-four pheasants rose on the wing right in front of us. I fired, and two-thirds of them dropped dead at my feet. Then the duke had a shot at what were left, and brought down three twenty-fourths of them, wounded in the wing. Now, out of those twenty-four birds, how many still remained?"

It seems a simple enough question, but can the reader give a correct answer?

106.

Every Saturday in the four bedroomed Nomad house, the four occupants, one to each room, change bedrooms so that only one of them keeps the same room. On one particular Friday, Arnie occupied the front left bedroom, Barbara the front right one, Carrie the back left and Denzil the back right. The next day, they changed rooms just before the landlord called for the rent. When he demanded his money, each made a statement about the location of the rent.

1. "The room to my right," said Arnie.

2. "The room in front of me," claimed Barbara.

3. "The room to my left," said Carrie.

4. "The room diagonally to the right of mine," said Denzil.

The problem was, two of the tenants lied, while two told the truth.

Note In a statement, a liar may refer to a room that does not exist, such as one 'behind' or 'to the left' of a back left room. Can you give the new occupant in each room and state who had the rent?

107.

One morning when Bhanu uncle was sleeping in his room, suddenly a ball hit his window pane and it was broken. Bhanu uncle walks to the window and asks the watchman, who has broken the 'window pane', watchman told him that 4 boys were playing cricket over here, they might have done this. Then the watchman goes to nearby the locality and bring 4 boys infront of Bhanu uncle. "Who broke the window pane?" asked Bhanu uncle.

Ravi said; It wasn't me, Bhanu uncle.

Swami said; It was David, Bhanu uncle.

David said; It was Tanmay, Bhanu uncle.

Tanmay said; No, it wasn't me, Bhanu uncle.

"I know boys well enough to know when you all are telling the truth; said Bhanu uncle; and I am sure that only one of you have just told the truth. That also tells we, which one of you broke the window." Bhanu uncle was right. Only one boy was telling the truth.

Can you help Bhanu uncle in finding the culprit?

108.

A public distribution shop is known as ration shop which has food items at a lower price than the market. A ration shop in Saharanpur has listed 20 food items for the next distribution among the people which are below poverty line and these people have to choose any 7 of them. Samara, a villager of Saharanpur, notices that there are three categories of foods: carbohydrate rich (C), protein rich (P) and vitamin rich (V).

Among these 20 food items, some are both carbohydrate and vitamin rich but are not protein rich (CV type). PC type foods are both carbohydrate and protein rich but are not vitamin rich and PV type foods are both protein and vitamin rich but are not carbohydrate rich. Samara also notes that the total number of PC type foods is 2 less than PV type foods. Similarly, the total number of PV type foods is 2 less than CV type and there is only 1 common food (CPV) across three categories. Furthermore, the number of only protein rich foods is same as only carbohydrate rich foods, but less than the number of only vitamin rich foods. Each food has at least one registration and there is at least one food in each category or combinations of categories.

Samara prefers C type foods and wants to avoid P type foods. She noted that the number of only C type food is 3. Ramesh's preference is V type foods followed by P type foods.

However, they want to take as many common foods as possible. What is the maximum number of foods that can be common between them, without compromising their preferences?

109.

Gandhi Maidan, Patna is a circular field with the inner radius of 5 km and outer radius of 10 km was divided into five successive stages for modernisation. The modernisation of each stage was handed over to different contractors.

1. Contractors are referred to the symbols C_1, C_2, C_3, C_4 and C_5.

2. The points between different stages of project are referred to the symbols P_1, P_2, P_3, P_4 and P_5 not necessarily in the same order.

3. Contractor C_5 was given the work of modernising stage starting at point P_4.

4. The stage from point P_5 to point P_3 was not the 1st stage.

5. Contractor C_4 was given the work of the 4th stage.

6. Stage 3 finished at point P_1 and the work of which was not given to contractor C_1.

7. Contractor C_3 was given work of stage ending at point 5.

Can you determine the starting and finishing points of stage 2?

110.

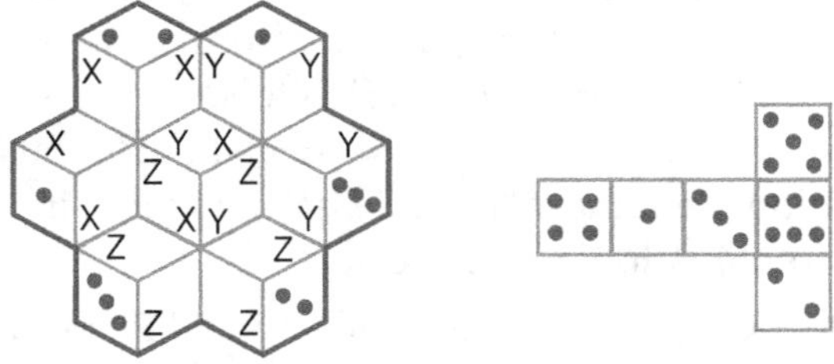

Position the missing pips on the seven standard dice of this puzzle. Do this in such a way that each of the three six-pointed stars which are identified by the letters 'X', 'Y' and 'Z' contain all six pip patterns. The illustrated foldout of a standard die must be used in solving the puzzle.

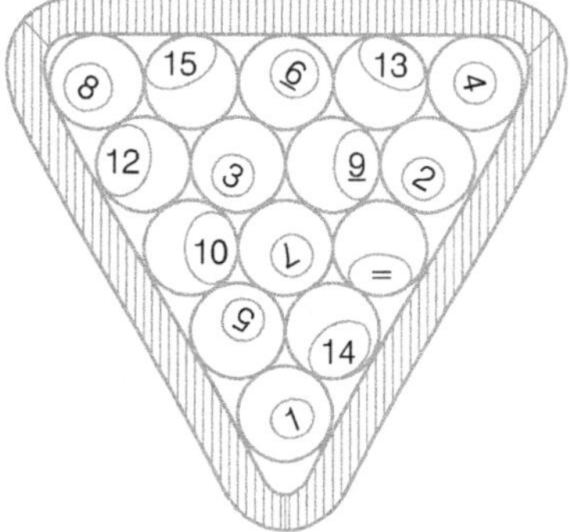

111.

An interesting game of pool involving three players has just been completed. It has a winner but the total point scores are as close as possible. Determine how the balls were distributed from the following information:

1. Each player has a different number of balls.

2. No player has two balls of consecutive number.

3. No player has two balls of identical colour.

Balls and their colours: 1 and 9 are yellow, 2 and 10 are blue, 3 and 11 are red, 4 and 12 are purple, 5 and 13 are orange, 6 and 14 are green, 7 and 15 are maroon and 8 is black.

112.

At airport, Indian delegates are saying good bye to American delegates, but it is not known who is leaving and who is staying. Each of the members of Indian delegation says farewell to each of the members of American delegates. Two say good bye, two men shake hands, but a man and a woman kiss once on the cheek and so do two women. A news reporter to the event counted 21 handshakes and 34 kisses.

Can you tell us how many men and women were saying good bye to each other?

113.

Most of the people solve this riddle immediately or it gives them really hard time. Although it might seem that solution doesn't exist don't give up. When you figure it out you'll be surprised how easy it is. How will YOU do in this puzzle?

Evil warlock doesn't like dwarfs so he chooses four of them and buries them into the ground so that only their heads are above surface. Dwarfs can't move at all and they can look only forward.

They're buried in a line and one of them is separated by a wall. They are all facing the same direction: last dwarf sees two heads of his friends and a wall. Second last sees only one head and a wall. Second dwarf sees only the wall and first is looking to the distance where he can see nothing interesting though.

Warlock explains the situation of dwarfs and tells them that he has placed hats on their heads–two blue hats and two red ones. One of the dwarfs is supposed to say what colour is the hat he is wearing. If he says the right colour warlock will dig them out immediately. If he says something else all of them will stay there till the end....

How will dwarfs solve this problem?

114.

Five International publishers came to showcase their books in World Book Fair. Each of the five publishers Princeton, Johnson, Holyfaith, Reprographics and Penguin published the book for competitive examinations. Each book contains three subjects among Geography, Science, History, Polity and Mental Ability. These books are arranged one over the other three of these are second editions and two of these are first editions. The book published by reprographic is the first edition.

The three books containing Science are stacked one over the other and both the first edition are stacked one over the other. All the second editions contain History. Neither of the first editions contain History. The book published by Holyfaith publishers contains Polity and Mental Ability. The book published by Princeton publisher is at the top of the stack and the book published by the Penguin publishers contains Mental Ability and Geography. There is no book which contains both Science and Geography.

Can you determine books of which publishers are on polity?

115.

There are four high income jewellery shops in Kochi namely Joyallukas, Emperor, H Samuel and Park Jewellers. The total amount of money with Joyallukas and Emperor together is equal to the total amount of money with H Samuel and Park together. But the total amount of money with Emperor and Park together is more than the amount of money with Joyallukas and H Samuel together. The amount of money with Joyallukas is more than that with Emperor.

Can you determine which jeweller has least amount of money?

116.

Each of the nine squares in the grid marked 1A to 3C should incorporate all the lines and symbols which are shown in the squares of the same letter and number immediately above and to the left. For example, 2B should incorporate all the lines and symbols that are in square 2 and square B.

One of the squares is incorrect. Which is it?

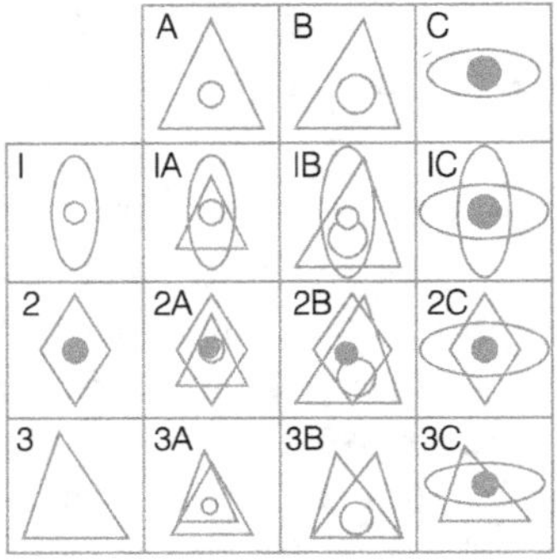

117.

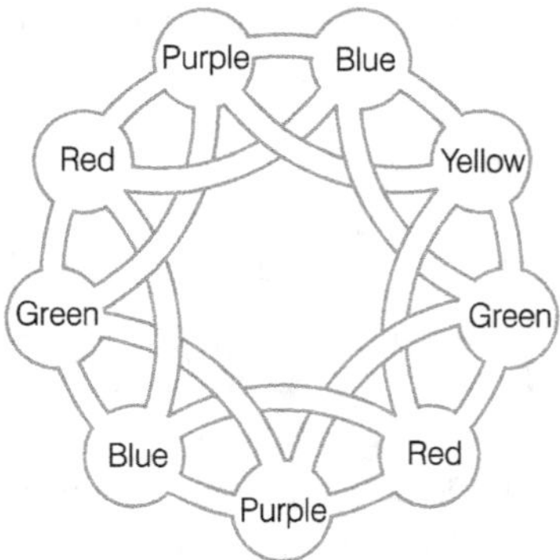

The interior lines of this puzzle crisscross but do not intersect. Place the numbers one through nine in the nine coloured circles to fulfil the following requirements:

1. Any set of three numbers which total fifteen (there are eight) must include three different colours.

2. Numbers of consecutive value may not be directly linked by any passage.

118.

	Male	Female	Location	Action
1.	Butch	Polly	Bridge	Danced
2.	Spike	Tania	Lake	Laughed
3.	Monty	Coriander	Field	Cried
4.	Quentin	Sylvia	Shop	Argued
5.	Norman	Daisy	River	Sneezed
6.	Henry	Bonny	Cinema	Whistled

The Spotty children were playing a game of Consequences where one suggested a male name, another a female name, a third gave a location where they met, and the last said what action they performed on meeting. On completing the game, the children voted on their favourite combination. The results are shown above but they have been recorded incorrectly. Each item is in the correct column, but only one item in each column is correctly positioned. The following facts are true about the correct order.

(1) Quentin in one place above Bonny.

(2) Laughed in one place below Tania but one above Monty.

(3) Shop was two places below Spike but three below Coriander.

(4) Spike is not adjacent to Norman.

(5) Field is one place below sneezed.

(6) Norman is one place above whistled but two below bridge.

(7) Polly is one place above Argued but three above river.

Can you give the correct male, female, location and action for each position?

119.

Generally, we come across so many sequence in our life and it's very easy to solve them, if we are able to recognise the pattern which they are following. But sometimes it becomes very difficult to solve something toughest of the sequence. We have presented a sequence below.

Can you tell which number would replace the 'X' in the given sequence?

1, 1, 2, 1, 3, 2, 4, 1, 5, 3, 6, 2, 7, 4, 8, 1, 9, 5, 10, 3, 11, 6, 12, 2, 13, 7, 14, 4, 15, 8, 16, 1, 17, 9, 18, 5, 19, 10, 20, 3, 21, 11, 22, X

120.

There are 16 shelves on a wall which are arranged as shown in the diagram below. On each shelf there is a tin of paint, each containing a different type of Yellow. Using the following information, see if you can determine which type of Yellow paint is on each of the 16 shelves.

1. Amber is below Fallow which is to the left of Cream and Topaz.
2. Sulphur is below Buff and to the left of Primrose.
3. Cream is below Xanthic which is also to the left of Primrose.
4. Lemon and Guilded are to the right of Gold which is below Topaz.
5. Gamboge is to the left of Plain Yellow and above Aureate which is to the right of Sulphur.
6. Primrose is to the right of Aureate and below Gilt.
7. Saffron is above Lemon and below Gilt.

To the left or right of refers to paint tins in the same row. Above or below refers to paint tins in the same column.

1	2	3	4
5	6	7	8
9	10	11	12
13	14	15	16

121.

The police have arrested 6 criminals and are trying to establish which of them is the gang boss. The inspector carrying out the investigation made the suspects stand in front of him in a line-up (in the same order as in the table) and asked each of them four questions. Both the questions and answers are set out in the table below:

No.	Question	John	Julian	Igor	David	Peter	James
1.	Are you the gang boss?	NO	NO	NO	NO	NO	YES
2.	Is the boss standing to your left?	NO	YES	NO	NO	YES	NO
3.	Is the boss standing to your right?	NO	YES	YES	NO	YES	NO
4.	Is the boss standing next to you?	YES	YES	YES	YES	NO	NO

Each criminal lied exactly twice. Can you, on the basis of the above answers, identify the gang boss?

Note To the left of Igor stands David, and to his right, Julian.

122.

Mr. Clinton received a call from his aunt Catherine that he will be visited by his aunt next week. On her arrival, Mr. Clinton introduced his five kids to Mrs. Catherine who had landed from Singapore. Mr./Mrs. Clinton displayed all five kids. First in line was Henry and then Victoria. When the aunt asked how old they were, Mr. Clinton said that the boy was exactly twice as old as girl. Then, Kathy walked in, who told that the combined age of Victoria and herself was twice that of Henry.

Then, the next kid, Sam came running in and all excited (possibly on account of the fact that he might receive some gifts), and the Mrs. Clinton remarked that the combined age of the two boys were exactly twice the combined ages of the two girls. The aunt has barely absorbed all these facts when Jenny entered the room and announced "Aunty you have actually arrived on my 21st birthday". "To this fact, Mr. Clinton finally added "The combined ages of my three girls is exactly equal to twice the combined ages of my two boys". What were the ages of the kids, according to these facts provided to the aunt Catherine of the kids?

123.

In a publication industry, there is a system of generating passcode for each batch, who starts there work in different time period. They have installed a coding machine, which generates passcodes for six batches everyday as follow:

Input You should know about type of questions.

Passcodes

Batch I You questions should of know type about.

Batch II About you type questions know should of.

Batch III About of you should type know questions, and so on till the six batch.

The first batch begins work at 10 : 00 am. Each batch works for one hour. There is a rest period of one hour after the fourth batch's work is over.

Can you determine, if the input on a day is "Eight friends are sitting in the circle," then what will be the passcode for the batch at 3 : 00 pm?

124.

Here's another test of your close reading and your ability to draw inferences from information. On Monday to Saturday last week, Opeyemi bought a reference book each day. The books are in one of two sizes, either large or small, as represented in the diagram below. Can you discover the subject of each book Opeyemi bought, as well as the day on which he bought it? The following clues contain all the information you'll need.

1. Opeyemi bought the thesaurus two days before he bought the large book (not the atlas), which is next to and left of the book on the subject of weather patterns and predictions.

2. The book purchased on Wednesday is larger than (and isn't next to) the one that covers the subject of cookery, which was bought two days later than the atlas.

3. The book on trees was bought before a small book that is next to the volume dealing with the recognition of insects, which Opeyemi bought earlier in the week than the book on trees.

4. He bought one of the large books on Saturday.

Book	Subject	Day

125.

A rather silly car thief stole, without knowing it, the car of the chief of police. The police immediately started an investigation and based on witness depositions, four suspects were arrested that were seen near the car at the time of the crime.

Because the chief of police took the case very seriously, he decided to examine the suspects personally and use the new lie detector of the police station. Each suspect gave three statements during the examinations, which are listed below:

Suspect A

1. "In high school, I was in the same class as suspect C."
2. "Suspect B has no driving licence."
3. "The thief didn't know that it was the car of the chief of police."

Suspect B

1. "Suspect C is the guilty one."
2. "Suspect A is not guilty."
3. "I never sat behind the wheel of a car."

Suspect C

1. "I never met suspect A until today."
2. "Suspect B is innocent."
3. "Suspect D is the guilty one."

Suspect D

1. "Suspect C is innocent."
2. "I didn't do it."
3. "Suspect A is the guilty one."

With so many contradicting statements, the chief of police lost track. To make things worse, it appeared that the lie detector did not quite work yet as it should, because the machine only reported that exactly four of the twelve statements were true, but not which ones.

Who is the car thief?

126.

In the land of Zoz, there live three types of person:

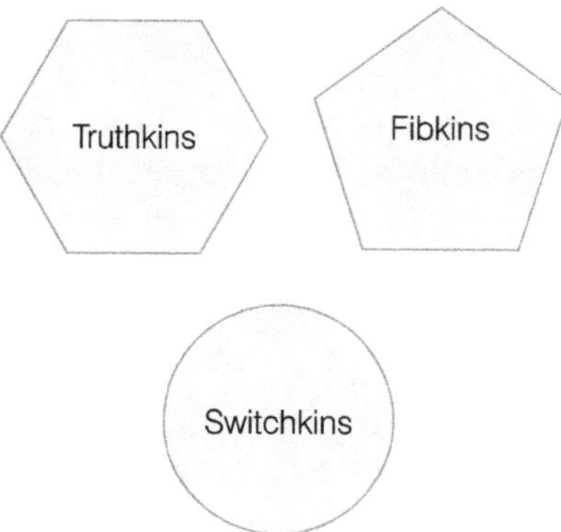

Truthkins, who live in hexagonal houses and always tell the truth;

Fibkins, who live in pentagonal houses and always tell lies; Switchkins, who live in round houses and who make true whatever they say.

One morning 90 of them gather in the city in three groups of 30. One group is all of one type; another group is made up evenly of two types; the third group evenly comprises three types. Everyone in the first group says, "We are all truthkins"; everyone in the second group says, "We are all fibkins" and everyone in the third group says, "We are all switchkins".

How many sleep in pentagonal houses that night?

127.

In a small village of Kashipur, people got divided into five groups on the basis of their religion. The groups head divided the village land into parts and made paths to travel from one place to another. No one was supposed to cross the blocks of land diagonally and was only allowed to move horizontally or vertically. Five men of different religions had to visit their religious places and were not allowed to cross the route of another not even their own. With the help of the picture of the paths, can you try to find the ways through which these men should move in order to reach their destination marked according to their number in the figure given?

			MAN 1			
	Place 4			Place 5		
			Place 3			MAN 4
		Place 2				MAN 2
				MAN 5		
MAN 3			Place 1			

Man 1 — Place 1

Man 2 — Place 2

Man 3 — Place 3

Man 4 — Place 4

Man 5 — Place 5

128.

In the faculty library, Robert and four other students are seated around the desk shown in the diagram below, all working very hard. Join them by studying these clues, to discover the name and surname (one of which is Holt) of the student in each seat, together with the subject he or she is reading about. The following clues contain all the information you'll need to complete the information table.

1. The five students are: Brian; the one reading a Biology book; the one surnamed Dart; the one (not Tina) reading a History book; and the person in seat A.

2. The five students are: Sue; the one reading a Chemistry book; the one surnamed Brown; the person in seat B; and the person in seat E.

3. Sue (whose surname isn't Jones) isn't sitting directly next to Brian.

4. Four of the students are: the one surnamed Fisher; the one reading an Art book; Louise; and the person in seat D.

5. Four of the students are: Louise; the one surnamed Jones; the one surnamed Brown (who isn't reading the Biology book); and the person in seat C.

6. Four of the students are: Sue (whose surname isn't Fisher); the student in seat A; the one reading a Geography book; and the one reading an Art book.

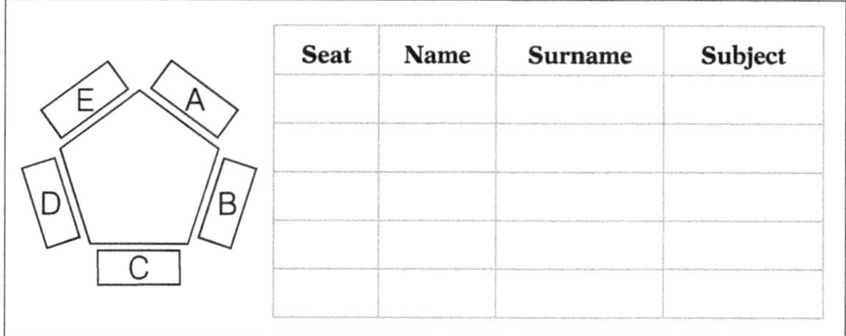

Seat	Name	Surname	Subject

129.

Integer m is the square of a certain two-digit number and it ends with 5. Is the third digit from last of this m number even or odd?

130.

A natural number was multiplied by 2 and the obtained product was increased by 1. Then, the obtained number was multiplied again by 2 and 1 was also added to the result.

The above two step operation was repeated five times. Can the final result be a number:

(a) divisible by 7?   (b) divisible by 12?

131.

Mr. Braclen, a Scotish farmer, was superstitious for his way of growing crops. He believed that if he grew two crops in the same field with a magic trick, then that would make him earn the maximum amount of money possible. One day he shared his trick with his son and said, if he will always grow two crops in a same rectangular field such that the ratio of the larger side of bigger rectangle to the smaller side is less than or equal to the ratio of sides of smaller rectangle, then it would make him earn more. Going by his father's secret, George decided to grow two crops in the manner shown in the picture.

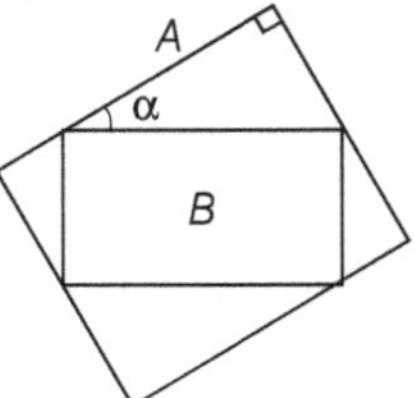

Here, rectangular field B is inscribed in rectangular field A, so that the corners of B is on a different sides of A. Can you find whether this way of dividing the field by son matches up with father's trick of maintaining a ration?

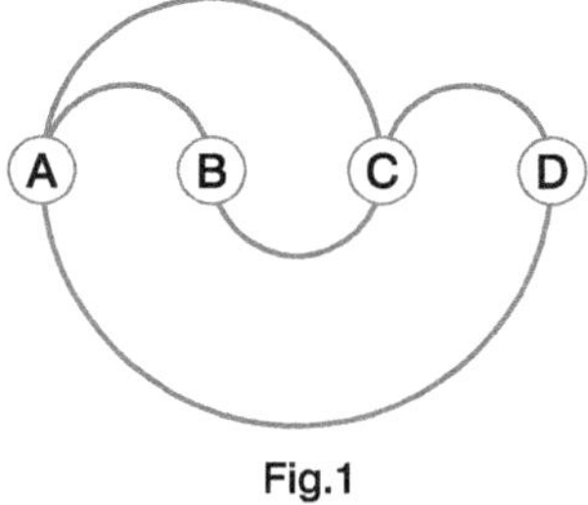

Fig.1

If one shape is divided in half, all three shapes would be identical.

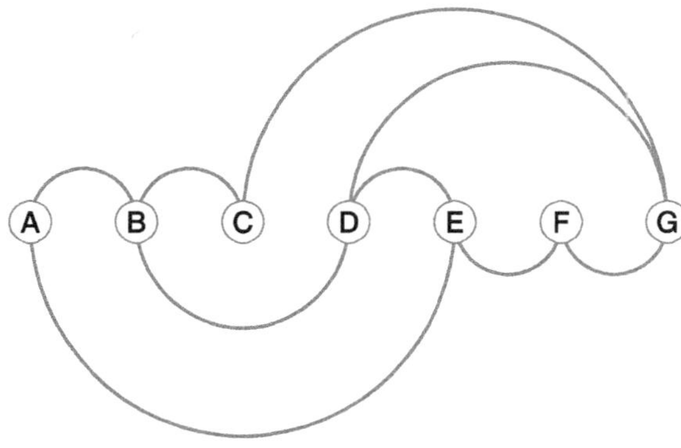

Fig. 2

All three shapes are identical.

Here are two distorted geometric figures. Both have been stretched in such a way that the original figure is unrecognisable at first glance. Your task is to straighten all the lines in each figure to reveal its original identity. The circled letters designate the intersection of two or more lines. Vital clues are given for each figure.

133.

Five men staying at a coastal hotel decide to go fishing on the pier. They sit next to each other, using different bait and catch different numbers of fish.

1. The plumber, called Henry, catches one fish fewer than Dick.
2. The electrician is next to the banker and uses bread for his bait.
3. The man at the North end of the pier is the banker, who is sitting next to Fred.
4. The salesman catches only one fish and is sitting at the South end of the pier.
5. Meal is the bait used by Malcolm and the man from Orlando catches 15 fish.
6. The man from New York uses shrimps for bait and is sitting next to the man who catches one fish.
7. Joe is from Los Angeles and uses worms as his bait.
8. The man in the middle is from Tucson and uses a bait of maggots.
9. The banker catches 6 fish.
10. Dick, who is the middle fisherman, is two seats away from the man from St Louis.
11. The man who is sitting next to the man from New York catches 10 fish and is a professor.
12. Henry did not sit next to Joe.

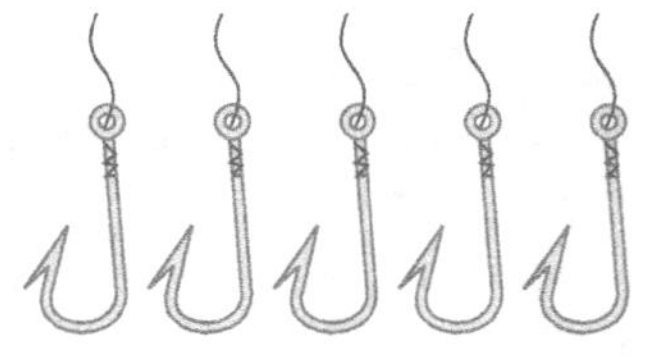

Work out where each man lives, his occupation, the bait he is using and how many fish he catches.

North ←——————————— Pier ——————————→ South

Name					
Occupation					
Town					
Bait					
Catch					

134.

	Creature	Home	Rise time	Cereal
1.	Otter	Reeds	6 am	Codflakes
2.	Toad	Sticks	8 am	Lice Krispies
3.	Newt	Boot	10 am	Flyflakes
4.	Perch	Dam	7 am	Pondpops
5.	Frog	Hollow log	9 am	Waterbix

Down at his local pond, Professor Hogweed was doing research into the breakfast habits of five pond creatures. He had listed the home, rising time and breakfast cereal of each creature in the order he had observed them but had managed to mix up the list when writing out a copy. Although the copied list shown had each item in the correct column, only one item was correctly positioned in each column. The following facts are true about the correct order:

(1) The creatures that lived in the sticks and the dam are not third and neither is the Lice Krispies eater.

(2) The Reeds resident is one place above the 9 am riser.

(3) The Pondpops diner is not last.

(4) The frog is two places above the 10 am riser.

(5) Neither the frog nor the perch are second.

(6) The newt is two places below the Lice Krispies diner.

(7) The Flyflakes diner is two places above the dam resident.

(8) Neither the 6 am nor the 9 am riser are fourth and neither is the reeds dweller.

Can you give the creature, home, rising time and breakfast cereal for each position?

135.

The puzzle is to place a different number in each of the ten squares so that the sum of the squares of any two adjacent numbers shall be equal to the sum of the squares of the two numbers diametrically opposite to them. The four numbers placed, as examples, must stand as they are. The square of 16 is 256 and the square of 2 is 4. Add these together and the result is 260. Also, the square of 14 is 196 and the square of 8 is 64. These together also make 260. Now, in precisely the same way, B and C should be equal to G and H (the sum will not necessarily be 260), A and K to F and E, H and I to C and D, and so on, with any two adjoining squares in the circle.

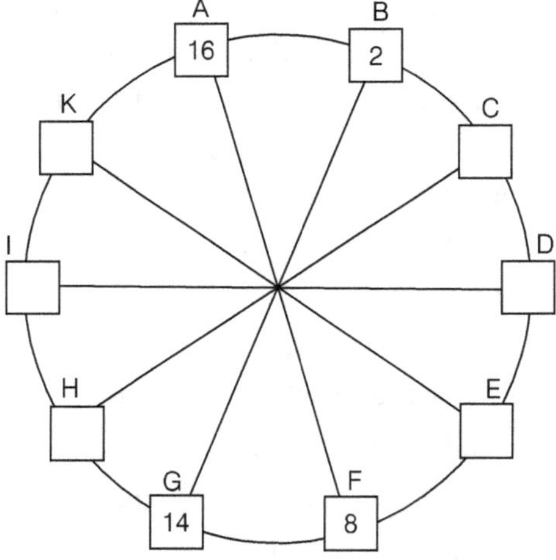

All you have to do is to fill in the remaining six numbers. Fractions are not allowed and I shall show that no number need contain more than two figures.

136.

In the summer resort of Bleakpale, there were exactly four guest houses standing in a line along the seafront. Business was grim and each guest house had only one guest with each guest house run by only one landlord.

1. The landlord of Kestrelview did not live next door to his fellow landlord Bob.

2. Harry stayed at one of the end guest houses, which was not Ivorytowers.

3. Daniel, who ran the guest house just to the right of where Frances was staying, was next door to the Lavender guest house which was not at the end of the line.

4. Eunice stayed next door to Ivorytowers.

5. Bob ran the guest house next door to where Harry was staying.

6. Arthur ran a guest house that had only one guest house next door, the one where Eunice was staying.

7. Colin, Geraldine and Jollyjapes were the remaining landlord, guest and guest house.

Numbering the guest house positions 1-4 from left to right, can you find the landlord, guest and guest house name for each position?

137.

Four identical circles intersect in such a way that the length of each shorter arc equals 3 inches. What is the circumference of each circle?

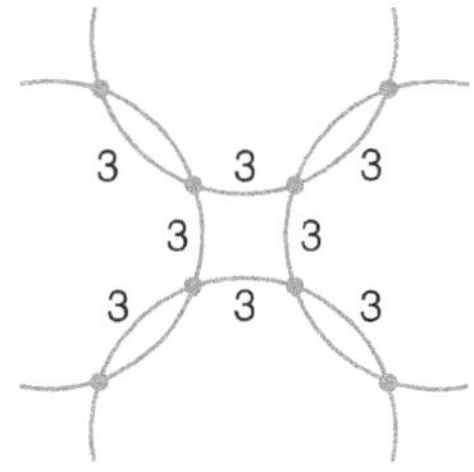

138.

Fit the nine small squares into the diagram to form a large square, each row and column of which should contain the letters a, b, c, d, e, f, g, h, i and j. What are the nine missing letters and in which order should they be placed into grid E?

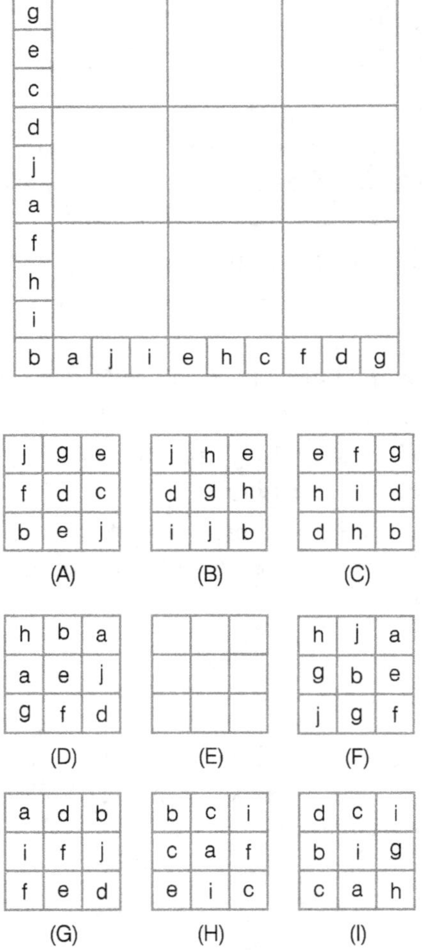

139.

My friend, Archibald, has moved into a new house in a long road in which the houses are numbered consecutively, 1-82. To find out his house number I ask him three questions to which I receive a yes/no answer. I will not tell you the answers, but if you can work them out you will discover his house number. The questions are:

1. Is it under 41? 2. Is it divisible by 4?

3. Is it a square number?

Can you work out the number of Archibald's house?

140.

Many years ago, in the days of the smuggler known as 'Rob Roy of the West,' a piratical band buried on the coast of South Devon a quantity of treasure which was, of course, abandoned by them in the usual inexplicable way. Some time afterwards its whereabouts was discovered by three countrymen, who visited the spot one night and divided the spoil between them, Giles taking treasure to the value of £ 800, Jasper £ 500 worth and Timothy £ 300 worth. In returning they had to cross the river Axe at a point where they had left a small boat in readiness. Here, however, was a difficulty they had not anticipated. The boat would only carry two men, or one man and a sack, and they had so little confidence in one another that no person could be left alone on the land or in the boat with more than his share of the spoil, though two persons (being a check on each other) might be left with more than their shares. The puzzle is to show how they got over the river in the fewest possible crossings, taking their treasure with them. No tricks, such as ropes, 'flying bridges,' currents, swimming or similar dodges, may be employed.

141.

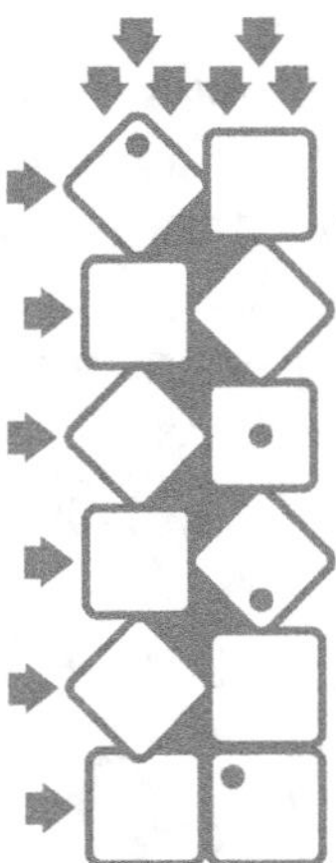

These six pairs of regulation dice have most of their pips missing. It is your task to position the missing pips to fulfil the following requirements:

(1) Each of the six stacked pairs of dice must total seven.

(2) Each of the six vertical pip columns pointed out by the six arrows at the top most also total exactly seven pips.

(3) Both vertical towers of six dice must reveal all faces, one through six.

142.

To remember certain codes or passwords, such as the PIN number, it is advisable to establish relationships between the digits that make them up since it has been noticed that such relationships tend to be retained in our memory much longer than the numbers themselves. Bill noticed that in his four-digit cell phone PIN, the second digit (counting from the left) is the sum of the last two digits and the first is the quotient of the last two. Moreover, the first two digits and the last two are made up of two two-digit numbers whose sum equals 100. Find Bill's cellular phone PIN.

143.

Philips electronics company which manufactures LED bulbs got a consignment to provide 3000 bulbs to Xerox company. The manufacturing site of the Philips company is 1000 km away from Xerox's godown. So, the manager decided to deliver the consignment on two trucks having a capacity of carrying 1000 bulbs each. But the transportation department informed that only one truck is available at present to carry the goods. While travelling towards the destination a bulb gets broken in every 1 km. So, can you find the largest number of bulbs that can be safely delivered to the Xerox company?

144.

There are three Federation Officers assigned to take three hostile aliens to 'Peace Talks' on another planet. However, they must follow the following rules:

- They have only one small space ship.
- Only two individuals can ride in the space ship each time.
- All Federation Officers can pilot the space ship, but only one alien can pilot the ship.
- If at any time there are both Federation Officers and aliens on a planet, then there must always be more (or the same number of) Federation Officers than aliens on that planet. This is because if there are more aliens than Federation Officers, then the aliens will kill the Federation Officers. Count any individual in the space ship when it is on one planet as being on that planet.
- The one space ship is the only means of transportation. There is no other way to get to the 'Peace Talks'. No one can exit the space ship while it is in flight.
- To start off, all the Federation Officers and aliens are on the same planet.

Can all Federation Officers and aliens get to the other planet alive, and if so, how?

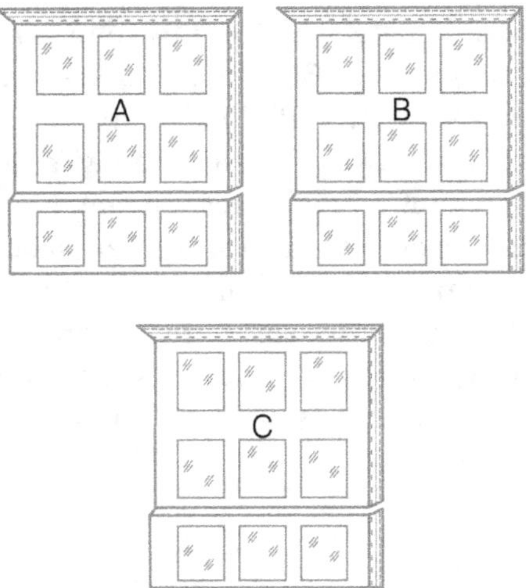

A man had in his office three cupboards, each containing nine lockers, as shown in the diagram. He told his clerk to place a different one-figure number on each locker of cupboard A, and to do the same in the case of B, and of C. As we are here allowed to call nought (zero, nil) a digit and he was not prohibited from using nought as a number, he clearly had the option of omitting any one of ten digits from each cupboard. Now, the employer did not say the lockers were to be numbered in any numerical order, and he was surprised to find, when the work was done, that the figures had apparently been mixed up indiscriminately. Calling upon his clerk for an explanation, the eccentric lad stated that the notion had occurred to him so to arrange the figures that in each case they formed a simple addition sum, the two upper rows of figures producing the sum in the lowest row. But the most surprising point was this: that he had so arranged them that the addition in A gave the smallest possible sum, that the addition in C gave the largest possible sum, and that all the nine digits in the three totals were different. The puzzle is to show how this could be done. No decimals are allowed and the nought may not appear in the hundreds place.

146.

Deepak always says, "I believe in creating leaders not followers." He applies this line in his day to day routine also as he never follows one way to office. He always takes new route to office. In the given figure, the line represents one way road allowing travel only Northwards or only Westwards.

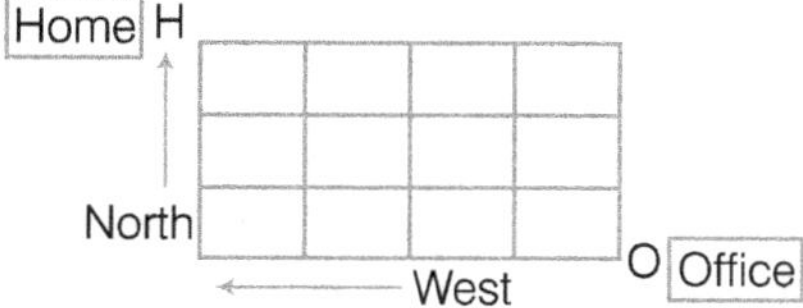

Can you determine in how many distinct routes can he reach home from office?

147.

The three coloured cards that Globule placed on the floor represented his prediction of the first three positions in next season's soccer league. Each card had a team written on its face-down side. On each uppermost face were two statements: one about that card's final league position (first, second or third) and one statement about the face-down teams.

The blue card claimed "This card has a league position somewhere above a card with a true positional statement" and "This card is neither Pity City nor Runaround Rovers," the green card said "This card is not adjacent in the league to a card with a false positional statement" and "One of the other cards is Definitely Disunited," and the red card stated "This card is neither second nor third" and "Runaround Rovers is not second." One of the cards had two true statements, one had two false and the other had one of each.

What were the first three positions?

148.

During an emergency in an area near the India-Pak border, the police commissioner decided to start the patrolling of the area to avoid any mishap. The police headquarters near the area planned to send PCR vans around the area. Each van has a fuel capacity to allow it to run half way around the whole area, along a great circle. The vans have the ability to refuel while running without loss of speed or spillage of fuel. Though, the fuel is unlimited, the area is the only source of fuel.

Find the fewest number of vans to get one van run all the way around the area assuming that all the vans must return safely to the police headquarters.

149.

Willie Wimper had just seen four men rob the Buckstown bank and had made a drawing of each man, marked A to D, for the police. The faces consisted of four rows of hair, eyes, noses and mouths. However, Willie had only managed to get one item correctly positioned in each row.

The following facts are true about the correct order:

1. Hair C is one place to the right of eyes C.
2. Eyes D are two places to the left of nose C, which is one to the right of mouth A.
3. Hair B is one place to the right of nose B, which is two places to the left of mouth D.

Can you correctly position the hair, eyes, nose and mouth of each robber?

150.

My five sisters, Erica, Lynne, Doreen, Claire and Marian, were late for work this morning, due to reasons beyond their control. Can you work out where each works, how late she arrived and the reason? These clues contain all the information you'll need.

1. Erica wasn't exactly 40 min late for work.
2. Lynne works in a store. The librarian (not Doreen or Erica) was exactly 30 min late for work.
3. The teacher (who was delayed from reaching the school by a violent hailstorm) was later for work than the women held up by strong winds.
4. Claire was 20 min later for work than the woman whose alarm clock failed to work (who wasn't exactly 20 min late). However, Claire wasn't as late as the woman who works in the theatre.
5. The woman who blamed black ice was 10 min later than the woman who had to make a lengthy detour to avoid a fallen tree.

	Workplace					Reason					Minutes late				
	Library	Office	School	Store	Theatre	Alarm clock	Black ice	Fallen tree	Hailstorm	Strong winds	20 min	30 min	40 min	50 min	60 min
Claire															
Doreen															
Erica															
Lynne															
Marian															
20 min															
30 min															
40 min															
50 min															
60 min															
Alarm clock															
Black ice															
Fallen tree															
Hailstorm															
Strong winds															

Name	Workplace	Reason	Minutes late

Explanations

1. The various spaces in the figure may be labelled as shown. The spaces P, Q, R have to be shaded by 3 different colours definitely (since, each of these 3 spaces lies adjacent to the other two). Now, in order that no two adjacent spaces be shaded by the same colour, the spaces T, U and S must be shaded with the colours of the spaces P, Q and R, respectively.

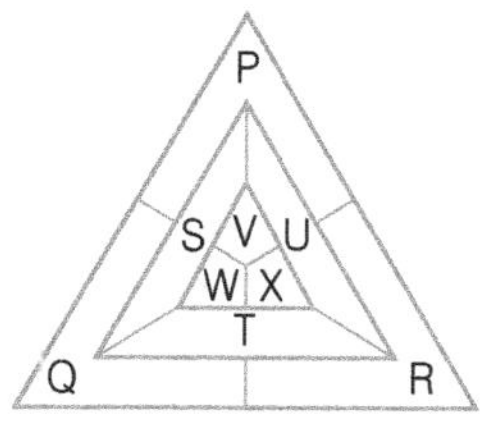

Also, the spaces X, V and W must be shaded with the colours of the spaces S, T and U, respectively i.e. with the colours of the spaces R, P and Q, respectively. Thus, the minimum 3 colours are required.

2. As,

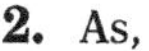

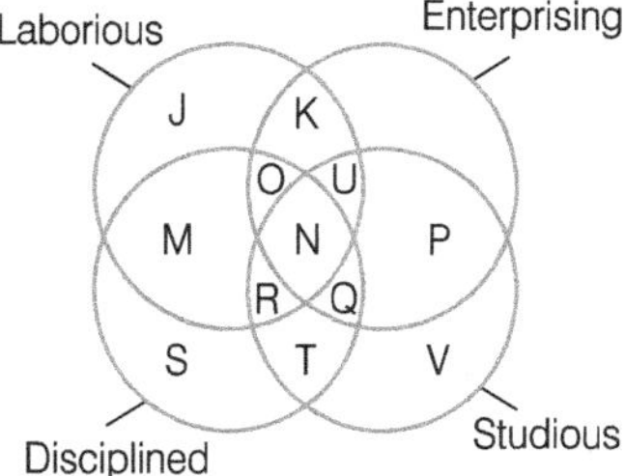

Here, we can make a table which will show the qualities of each person.

Persons	Qualities
K	Laborious, Enterprising
O	Laborious, Enterprising, Disciplined
P	Enterprising, Studious
U	Laborious, Enterprising, Studious
N	Laborious, Enterprising, Studious, Disciplined
R	Laborious, Disciplined, Studious,
Q	Disciplined, Studious, Enterprising
T	Disciplined, Studious
V	Only studious
S	Only disciplined
J	Only laborious
M	Disciplined, Laborious

So, from the table it is clear that only J has laborious quality.

3. There is only one way of finding a solution to this problem:

Numbers which leave a remainder of 1, when divided by 2 are 3, 5, 7, 9, 11, 13, 15, 17, 19, 21, 23, 25, 27, 31, 33, 35.

Numbers which leave a remainder of 1, when divided by 3 are 4, 7, 10, 13, 16, 19, 22, 25, 28, 31, 34, 37......

Numbers which leave a remainder of 1, when divided by 4 are 5, 9, 13, 17, 21, 25, 29, 33, 37.

Numbers which leave no remainder when divided by 5 are 5, 10, 15, 20, 25, 30, 35.

The only number fulfilling the four conditions is 25.

So, 25 eggs were broken.

4. Pablo Picaso made 4 master piece (1, 2, 3, and 4) as shown below

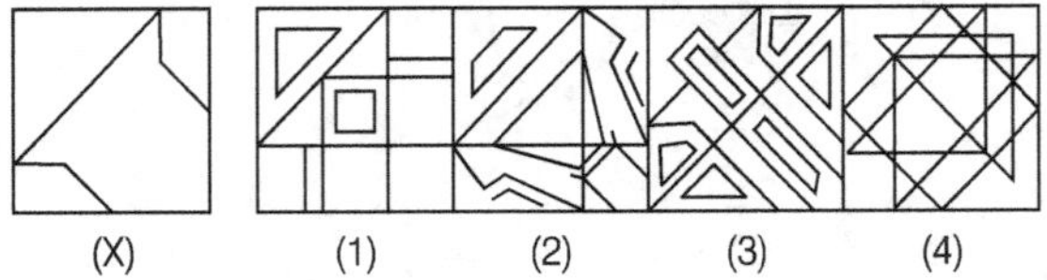

and asked one of his appreciator to find image (X) inscribed in these 4 figures (1, 2, 3 and 4).

Now, the image (X) is inscribed in figure number 4 as shown below.

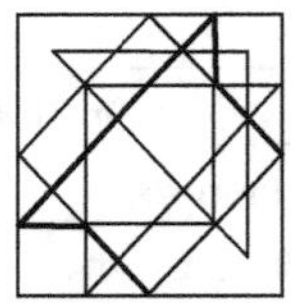

5. Major Samar Anand recognised the pattern in which this number appeared and cut the exact wire, the pattern is as follows

1st minute	2nd minute	3rd minute	4th minute	5th minute
589654237	89654237	8965423	965423	96542
↑ Remove	↑ Remove	↑ Remove	↑ Remove	

So, we can see that in the bomb, the digits are removed one by one from the beginning and the end alternately, so the number that could have appear to explode the bomb was 96542.

6. Given that, the length of the head = 9 cm

Then, he measured the tail and found that it was the length of the head plus half the length of body. So, it can be written as,

$$\text{Length of tail} = \text{head} + \frac{\text{body}}{2} \qquad \text{...(i)}$$

and
$$\text{Body} = \text{head} + \text{tail} \qquad \text{...(ii)}$$

From Eqs. (i) and (ii),

$$\text{Tail} = \text{head} + \frac{\text{head} + \text{tail}}{2}$$

$$2\,\text{Tail} = 2\,\text{head} + \text{head} + \text{tail}$$

$$2\,\text{Tail} = 3\,\text{head} + \text{tail}$$

$$\text{Tail} = 3\,\text{head}$$

$$\text{Tail} = 3 \times 9 \qquad \text{[given, head = 9 cm]}$$

$\therefore$ Length of tail = 27 cm

Putting the value of tail in Eq. (ii), we get

$$\text{Body} = \text{head} + 27$$

$$= 9 + 27$$

$\therefore$ Length of body = 36 cm

So, the length of fish = Length of body + Length of tail + Length of head

$$= 36 + 27 + 9$$

$$= 72\,\text{cm}$$

7. On opening the folded sheet of paper, the designer would get the following design of cut work.

Half unfold

On completely unfolding the paper, the exact cut work design will be as follows:

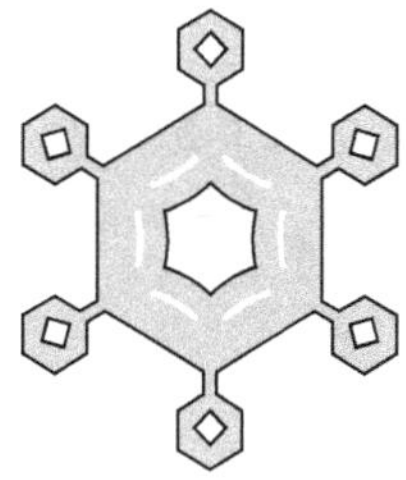

8. Indian parliament security system follows the following pattern in the three stages.

In stage 3,

$$20 + 15 = 35$$
$$35 + 15 = 50$$
$$50 + 15 = 65$$
$$\text{So, } ? = 65$$

In stage 2,

$$18 + 20 = 38$$
$$38 + 35 = 73$$
$$73 + 50 = 123$$
$$123 + 65 = 188$$
$$\text{So, } ? = 188$$

In stage 1,

$$2 + 18 = 20$$
$$20 + 38 = 58$$
$$58 + 73 = 131$$
$$131 + 123 = 254$$
$$254 + 188 = 442$$
$$\text{So, } ? = 442$$

So, the codes at third stage of security check will be 20, 35, 50, **65.**

9. According to the given information, six cars are parked in 2 rows in such a way that the front of 3 cars parked in row 1 is facing the other 3 cars in row 2, like this,

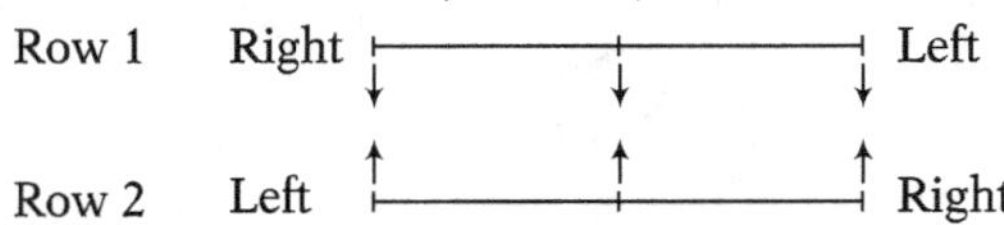

From condition (i): Alto is not parked in beginning of any row. So, Alto will be parked in the middle of any row as shown below

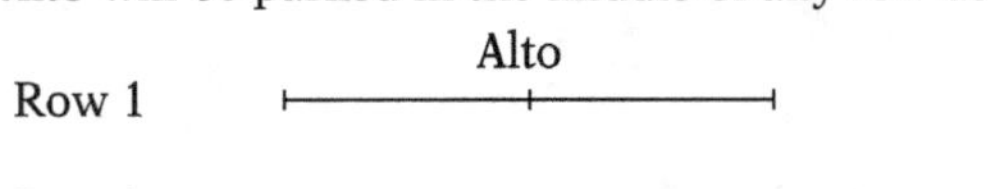

From condition (iv): Swift is parked in front of Alto, then arrangement will be as

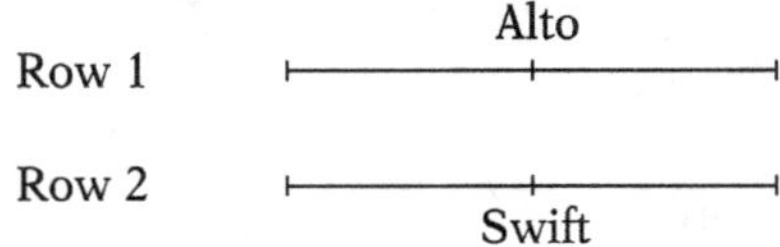

From condition (v): S X 4 is parked to the immediate right of Alto as shown below

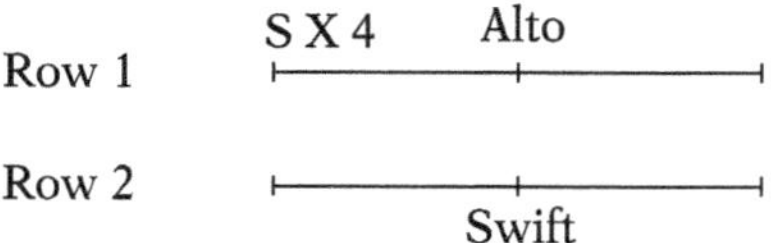

From condition (iii): Punto, which is the neighbour of Alto is parked diagonally opposite to i10 as shown below

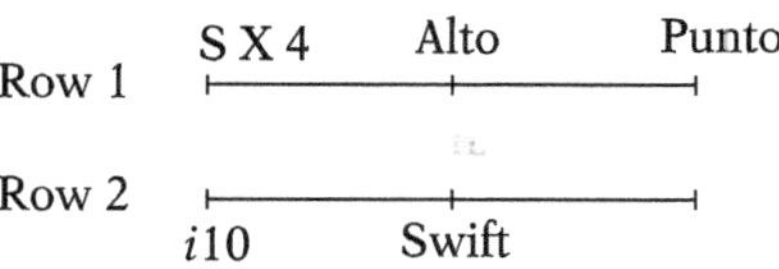

From condition (ii): Esteem is second to the right of i10 as shown below

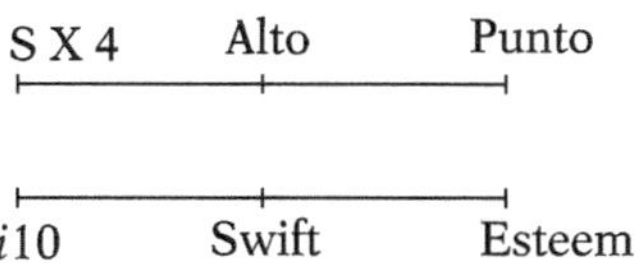

Now, if S X 4 and Esteem exchange their positions mutually, then Alto will be adjacent to Esteem.

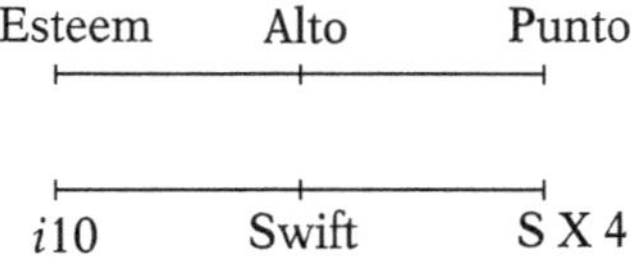

10. We shall label the various regions in the given figure as shown below

The regions A, C, E and G can have the same colour 1.

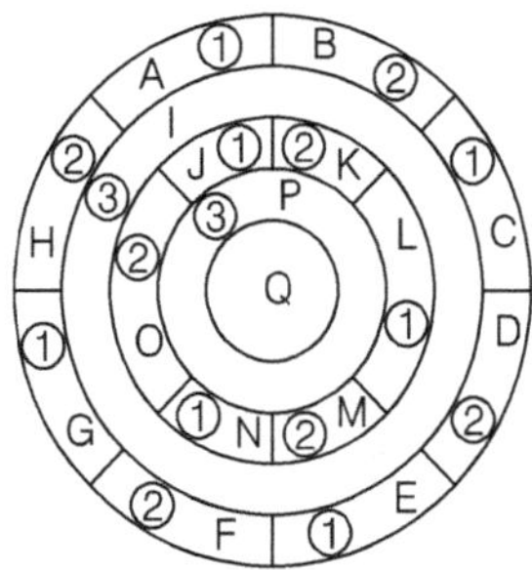

The regions B, D, F and H can have the same colour (but different from colour 1) say colour 2.

The region I lies adjacent to each one of the regions A, B, C, D, E, F, G and H and therefore it should have a different colour say colour 3.

The regions J, L and N can have the same colour (different from colour 3) say colour 1.

The regions K, M and O can have the same colour (different from the colours 1 and 3). Thus, these regions will have colour 2.

The region P can not have any of colours 1 and 2 as it lies adjacent to each one of the regions J, K, L, M, N and O and so it will have colour 3.

The region Q can have any of the colours 1 or 2.

$\therefore$ Minimum number of colours required is 3.

11. To find the numbers of first row of the second figure, add 5 to each number of the first row of the first figure as shown below

$$3 + 5 = 8$$
$$11 + 5 = 16$$
$$15 + 5 = 20$$

To find the numbers of the second row of the second figure, deduct 3 from the each number of the second row of the first figure as shown below

$$18 - 3 = 15$$
$$24 - 3 = 21$$
$$32 - 3 = 29$$

To find the numbers of the third row of the second figure, add 4 to each number of third row of the first figure as shown below

$$22 + 4 = 26$$
$$21 + 4 = 25$$
$$9 + 4 = 13$$

Same pattern will be follow in other two figures. So, the numbers in fourth figure are

18	26	30
9	15	23
34	33	21

Hence, option (c) is correct.

12. There are 49 possible combinations when rolling two 7 sided dice. There are still six ways of making a total of 7, therefore, the probability is $\dfrac{6}{7^2} = \dfrac{6}{49}$.

In each scenario, there are still only six ways of making a total of 7, the only thing that changes is the number of possible combinations.

The probability of total 7

on 7 sided dice $= \dfrac{6}{7^2} = \dfrac{6}{49}$

on 8 sided dice $= \dfrac{6}{64}$

on 9 sided dice $= \dfrac{6}{81}$

on 10 sided dice $= \dfrac{6}{100}$

13.

The pattern in above figure is as follows:

In the first row, the first three numbers add up to give the fourth number as shown below

$$1 + 5 + 7 = 13$$

Same pattern is followed in row III,

$$3 + 8 + 2 = 13$$

Now, in the second row, the second, third and fourth numbers are added to give the first number as shown below.

$$15 = 5 + 4 + 6$$

Same pattern is followed in row IV.

$$12 = 5 + 2 + ?$$
$$12 = 7 + ?$$
$$? = 5$$

So, the missing number is 5.

14.

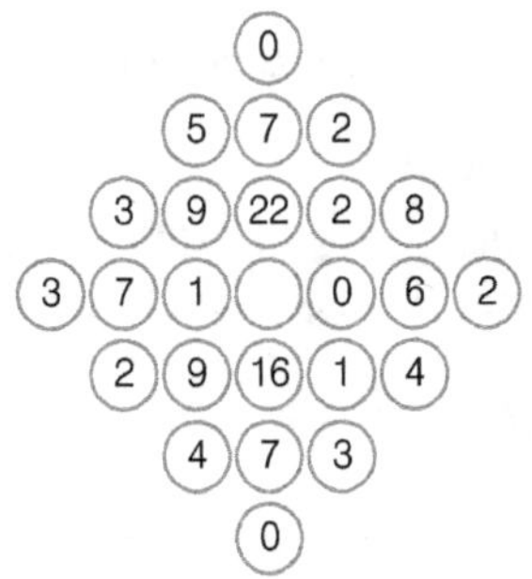

The pattern in the figure is as follows

$$5 + 2 = 7$$
$$3 + 9 + 2 + 8 = 22$$
$$3 + 7 + 1 + 0 + 6 + 2 = 19$$
$$2 + 9 + 1 + 4 = 16$$
$$4 + 3 = 7$$

The circle in the central column equal to the sum of the numbers in each corresponding row. So, the value of centre circle will be 19.

15. Sorting out the four designs what Addison got are shown below:

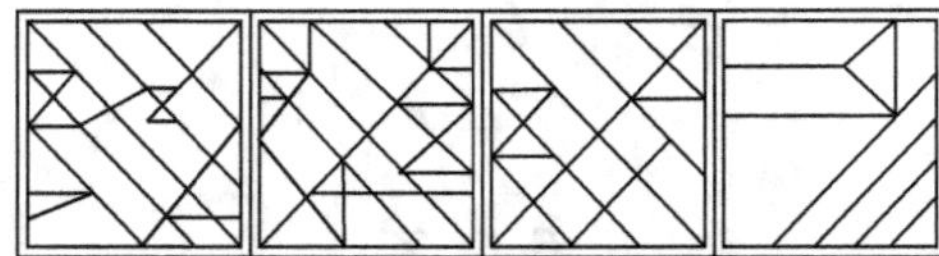

Looking into the four figures, it can be realised that the design in figure (a) includes the part of design which Addison's father could capitulate.

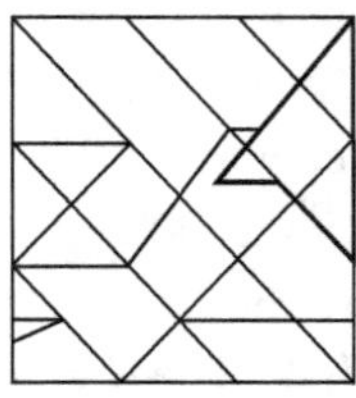

So, hotel having design of figure (a) is the place where Addison's father parked his car.

16. From statement II,

The body of the driver was not recovered. So, it is clear that either driver died or escaped in the accident.

Hence, the answer would be either conclusion I or II follows. Therefore, possibility III is valid.

17. According to the representatives,

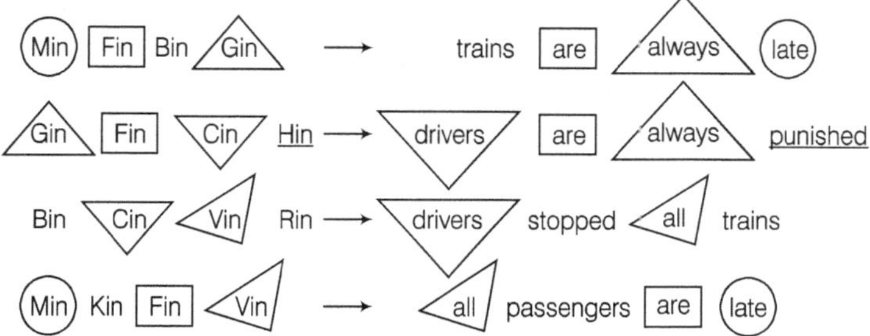

From the above, we get

$$Hin \longrightarrow Punished$$
$$Fin \longrightarrow Are$$
$$Kin \longrightarrow Passengers$$
$$Vin \longrightarrow All$$
$$Gin \longrightarrow Always$$
$$Min \longrightarrow Late$$

'Hin Fin Kin' means 'Punished Are Passengers'.

Or

'Hin Fin Kin' means 'Passengers Are Punished'.

18. (b) In each row, add the black squares from the left hand and centre boxes to give the figure in the right hand box. So, option (b) is correct.

19. Tighten two ropes between corners of a square. Put one ring on each rope and tighten another rope between them. That rope goes through the ring on sheep's neck.

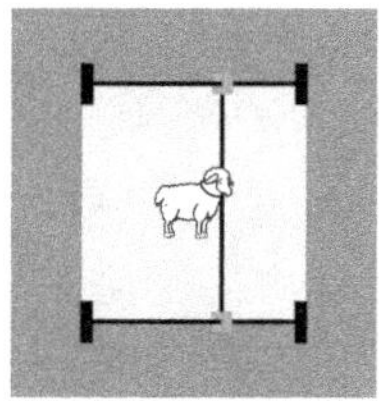

20. From the first figure of row 1, if we rotates it by 180° around its central point, then we get the same figure as shown below.

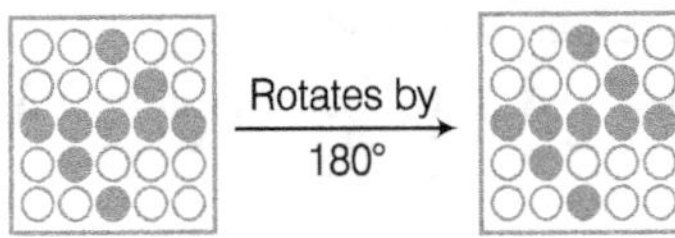

Same pattern is followed in other figures. So, figure in option (e) is rotationally symmetrical by 180° around its central point as shown below.

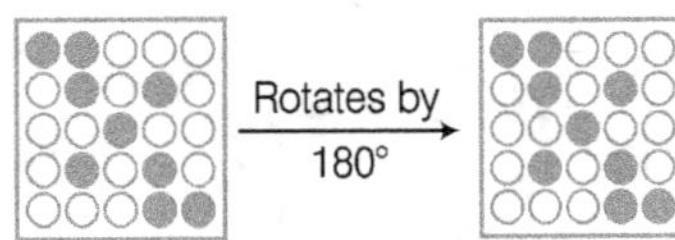

Hence, option (e) is correct.

21. In the I row, the pattern is as follows:

$$2 + 14 = 16$$
$$16 - 6 = 10$$
$$10 - 9 = 1$$
$$1 + 7 = 8$$
$$8 - 15 = -7$$

Similarly,

In the II row,

$$10 + 14 = 24$$
$$24 - 6 = 18$$
$$18 - 9 = 9$$
$$9 + 7 = 16$$
$$16 - 15 = 1$$

In the III row,

$$33 + 14 = 47$$
$$47 - 6 = 41$$
$$41 - 9 = 32$$
$$32 + 7 = 39$$
$$39 - 15 = 24$$

In the IV row,

$$17 + 14 = 31$$
$$31 - 6 = 25$$
$$25 - 9 = 16$$
$$16 + 7 = 23$$
$$23 - 15 = 8$$

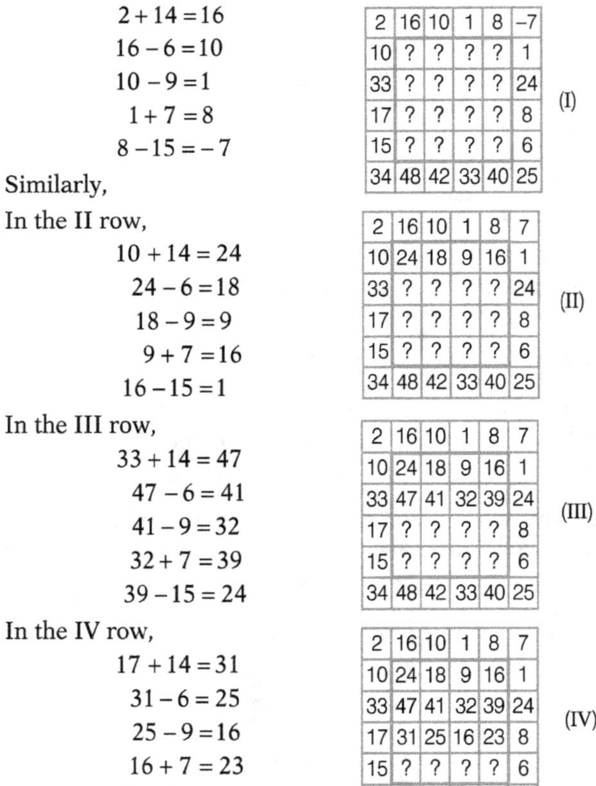

(I)

2	16	10	1	8	-7
10	?	?	?	?	1
33	?	?	?	?	24
17	?	?	?	?	8
15	?	?	?	?	6
34	48	42	33	40	25

(II)

2	16	10	1	8	7
10	24	18	9	16	1
33	?	?	?	?	24
17	?	?	?	?	8
15	?	?	?	?	6
34	48	42	33	40	25

(III)

2	16	10	1	8	7
10	24	18	9	16	1
33	47	41	32	39	24
17	?	?	?	?	8
15	?	?	?	?	6
34	48	42	33	40	25

(IV)

2	16	10	1	8	7
10	24	18	9	16	1
33	47	41	32	39	24
17	31	25	16	23	8
15	?	?	?	?	6
34	48	42	33	40	25

In the V row,

$$15 + 14 = 29$$
$$29 - 6 = 23$$
$$23 - 9 = 14$$
$$14 + 7 = 21$$
$$21 - 15 = 6$$

2	16	10	1	3	7
10	24	18	9	16	1
33	47	41	32	39	24
17	31	25	16	13	8
15	29	23	14	21	6
34	48	42	43	40	25

(V)

So, the missing section will be like this

24	18	9	16
47	41	32	39
31	25	16	23
29	23	14	21

Hence, option (d) is correct.

22. Matthew was sitting to the right of Agatha, so Kevin must have been sitting to her left side. To the left of Kevin might have been sitting either Celine or Daphne (we do not take Barbara into account as she is Kevin's wife).

Let's consider both the cases:

(a) If it was Celine sitting to the left of Kevin, then to her left must have been John (Kevin and Matthew are already sitting elsewhere, and Leon is Celine's husband). We know that, Daphne was also sitting next to John, so she must have taken a seat to his left. The remaining two seats were occupied by Leon and Barbara (see figure beside), which means that to the right of Barbara was Leon.

(b) If it was Daphne sitting to the left of Kevin, then as per the guidelines of the problem, to her left side John sat. The next three seats were occupied by: Barbara, Celine, and Leon: Leon was sitting between Barbara and Celine (otherwise the two ladies would have been sitting next to each other)-see figure on the right.

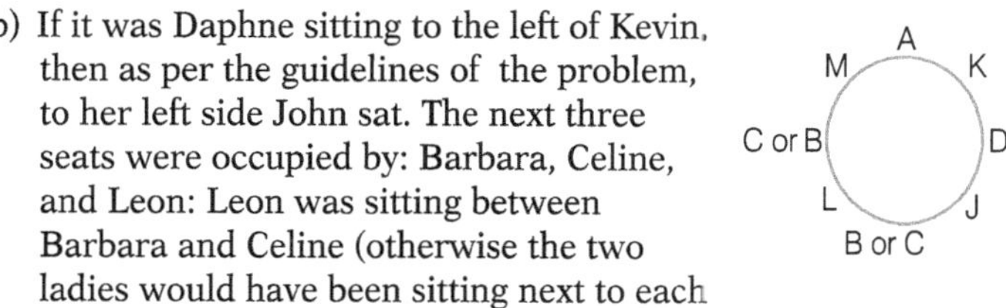

In that case, however, Celine would have, then been neighbouring on her husband, Leon. This case is, therefore, rejected as being impossible. Hence, Leon sat to right of Barbara.

23. There are 8 representatives A, B, C, D, E, F, G and H from 8 different countries *viz*-Thailand, France, Holland. Austria, US, Spain, India and Germany (not necessarily in the same order). According to the given information, we can get the final arrangement by following the given steps as shown below:

Step 1- A, who represents Germany, sits 3rd to the left of E, then arrangement is as following

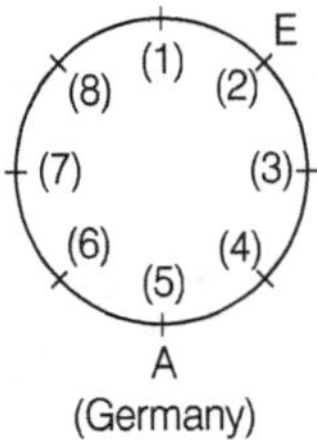

Step 2- In step 2, the one who is from India sits on the immediate right of A, then arrangement is as following

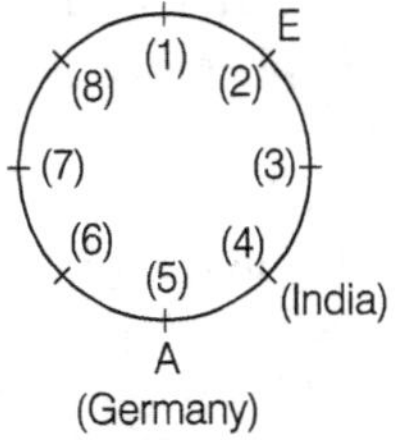

Step 3- D who is from Holland, sits 2nd to the right of B. B is not an immediate neighbour of E. So, B can not sit at position (1) and (3), then B will sit at position (8) as shown in arrangement below

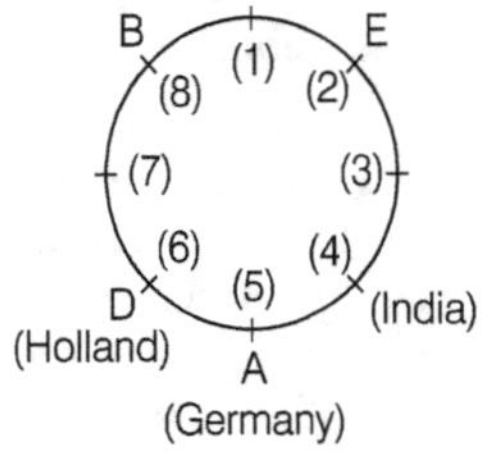

Step 4- C, who is from Spain, sits exactly in the middle of people representing US and India. So, E will be from US as shown in arrangement below

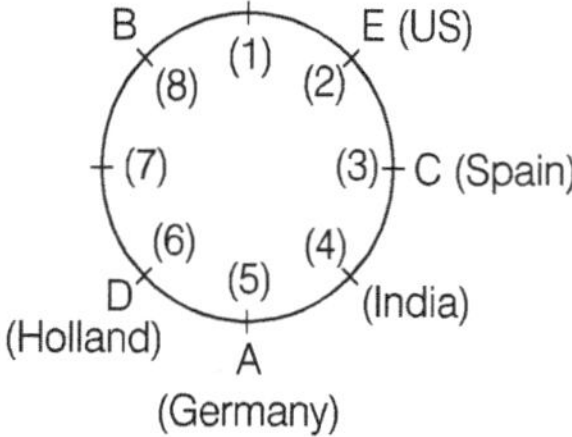

Step 5- G, who is the representative of France, sits 2nd to the left of H. Who is from Thailand , then G will be at position (1) and H will be at position (7).

F will be at position (4) and B will be from Austria as shown in final arrangement below

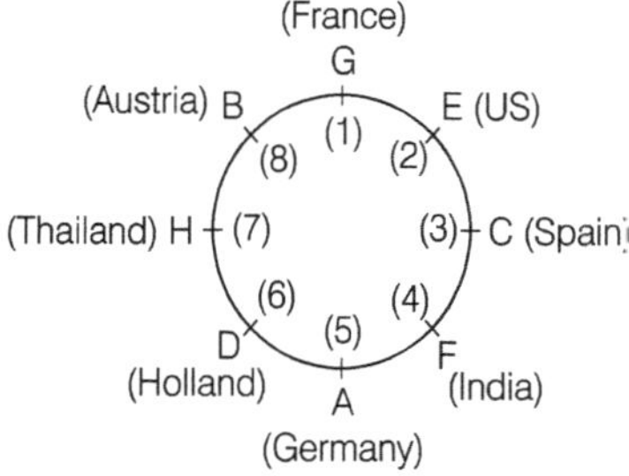

So, from the above arrangement, it is clear that the representative from Holland is seated second to the left of the Indian representative.

24. The route of minimum distance Subhash Ghai has to follow is

$$\text{Dharamshala} \xrightarrow[1\,km]{} \text{Kullu} \xrightarrow[2\,km]{} \text{Shimla} \xrightarrow[3\,km]{} \text{Manali} \xrightarrow[3\,km]{} \text{Mandi}$$

$$= (1 + 2 + 3 + 3) = 9\,\text{km}$$

25. In the 'Sunset vue' bar, where customers enjoy the 'Make A sum' game. Carlo has laid out the number coasters as below

39	13	32	11	24

= 109

There are four mathematical symbols $(+, -, \div, \times)$. You have to make a working sum (i.e. 109) by inserting these mathematical symbols between the coasters.

You can put the symbols in any order. Now, put the symbols in coaster like this,

| 39 | + | 13 | × | 32 | – | 11 | + | 24 |

| = | 109 |

$$= 39 \div 13 \times 32 - 11 + 24$$
$$= 3 \times 32 - 11 + 24$$
$$= 96 - 11 + 24$$
$$= 85 + 24$$
$$= 109$$

26. There are three bus routes 1, 2 and 3 between Anand Vihar and Faridabad.

According to given condition,

Route 1 has intermediate stops at Badarpur and Dilshad Garden

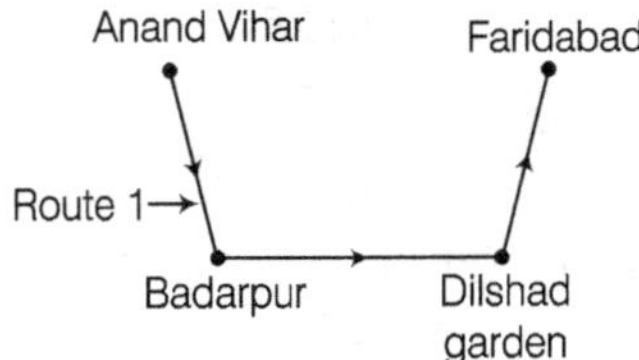

Route 2 has stops at Chanakyapuri and Dilshad Garden

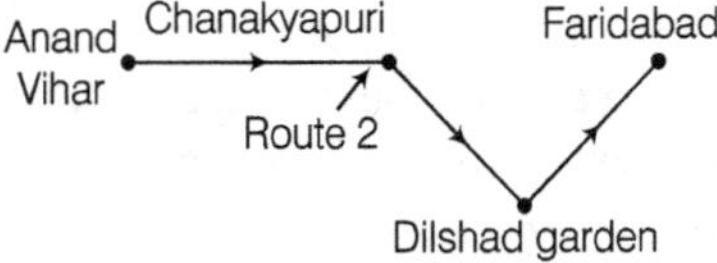

The shortest route 3 with a length of 10 km stops at Chanakyapuri only, which is exactly at the middle of this route .

Given that,

Distance between Chanakyapuri and Dilshad garden = 4 km

Badarpur and Dilshad garden = 3 km

Faridabad and Dilshad garden = 2 km

Now, combine all the routes together then, we get

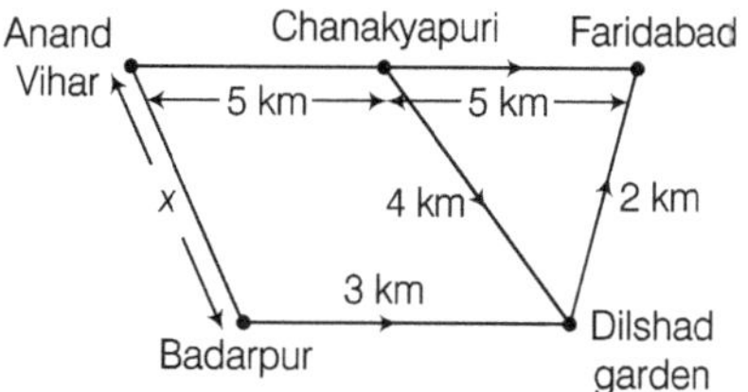

Let, the distance between Anand Vihar and Badarpur is x km. But given that the longest route has 3 km more length than the shortest route (route 3).

The length of shortest route 3

$$= A \xrightarrow{5} C \xrightarrow{5} F = 10 \text{ km}$$

where,   A → Anand Vihar

C → Chanakyapuri

F → Faridabad

B → Badarpur

D → Dilshad garden

The length of route 2 $= A \xrightarrow{5} C \xrightarrow{4} D \xrightarrow{2} F = 11$ km

So, route 2 can not be the longest route.

Now, the length of route 1 $= A \xrightarrow{x} B \xrightarrow{3} D \xrightarrow{2} F = x + 5$

and $x + 5 = 13$

$x = 8$ km

So, the distance between Anand Vihar and Badarpur $(x) = 8$ km

27. According to the given information, we can make a following venn diagram as shown below:

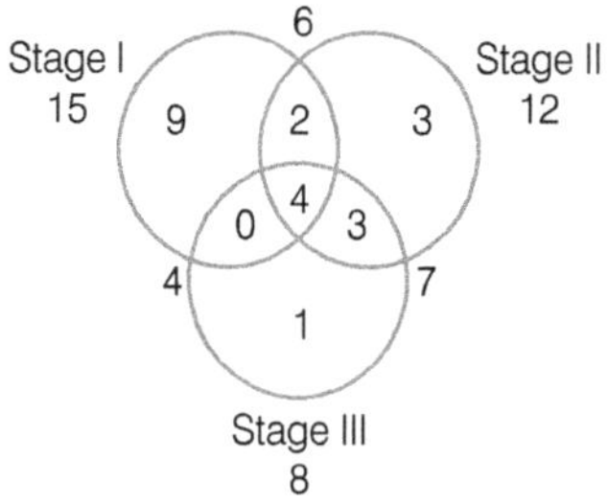

Let, number of failures of stage I $= A$

Number of failures of stage II $= B$

Number of failures of stage III $= C$

Given that,

Number of failures in stage I $= 15$

$$n(A) = 15$$

Similarly, in stages II and III,

$$n(B) = 12$$

$$n(C) = 8$$

According to the question, software failed 6 times in stage I and II. It can be written as $n(A \cap B) = 6$

Similarly, $n(B \cap C) = 7$

$$n(A \cap C) = 4$$

Software failed 4 times in stage I, II and III. It can be written as

$$n(A \cap B \cap C) = 4$$

Total number of single failure in stage I

$$= n(A) - n(A \cap B) - n(A \cap C) + n(A \cap B \cap C)$$

$$= 15 - 6 - 4 + 4 = 9$$

Total number of single failure in stage II

$$= n(B) - n(A \cap B) - n(B \cap C) + n(A \cap B \cap C)$$

$$= 12 - 6 - 7 + 4 = 3$$

Total number of single failure in stage III

$$= n(C) - n(B \cap C) - n(A \cap C) + n(A \cap B \cap C)$$

$$= 8 - 7 - 4 + 4$$

$$= 1$$

Thus, we can say that software failed in a single stage $= 9 + 3 + 1$

$$= 13 \text{ times}$$

28. The pattern is as follows:

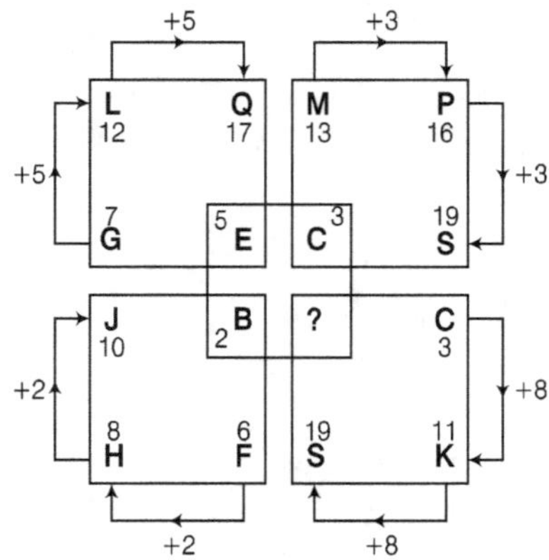

In the given figure, each square has the following sequence.

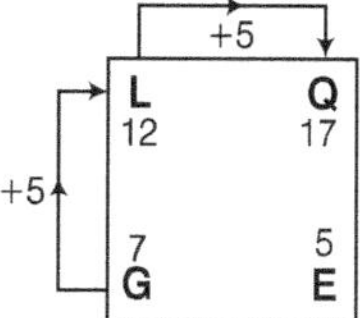

Now, the difference of the positional values of the letters is 5 and the alphabet related to positional value 5 is E.

Similarly, in the missing letter square, the difference of the positional values of the letters is 8 and the alphabet related to positional value 8 will be H.

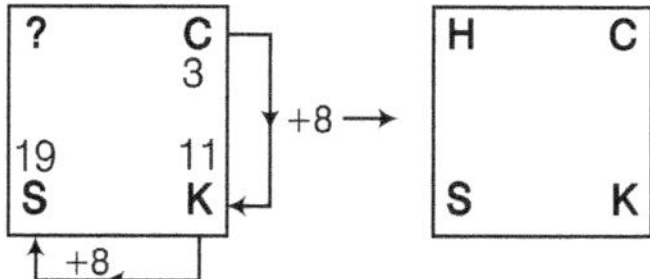

So, the ? is replaced by H.

29. In the given clock, the hour hand moves 3h clockwise and minute hand moves 20 min anticlockwise each time as shown below

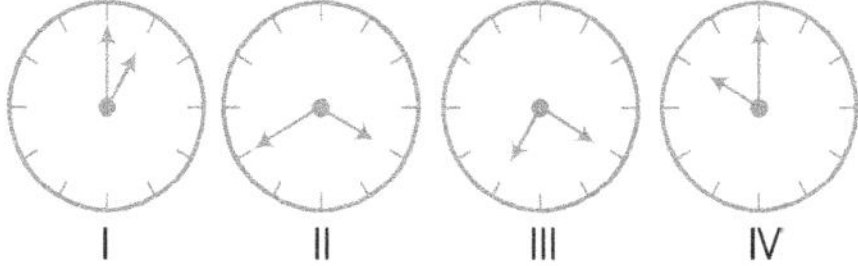

30. In the first row, the figure on the extreme right is formed by super imposing the extreme left hand figure rotated 90° clockwise and the centre figure rotated 90° anticlockwise as shown below

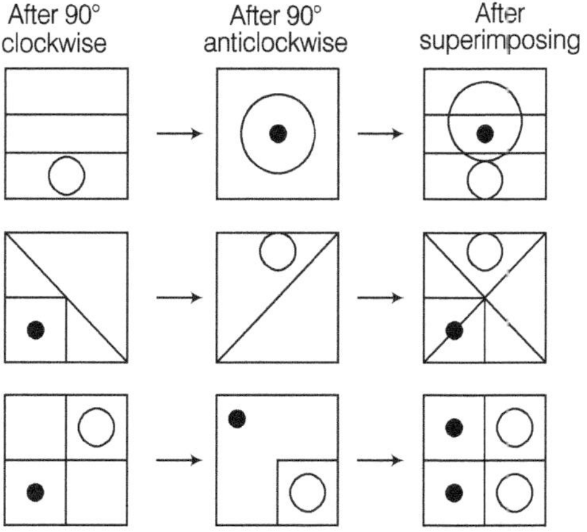

31. Let us assume that the initial length of both the candles was L and Ken read for T hours.

In T hours, total thin candle burnt $= \dfrac{TL}{3}$

In T hours, total thick candle burnt $= \dfrac{TL}{6}$

After T hours, total thick candle remaining $= L - \dfrac{TL}{6}$

After T hours, total thin candle remaining $= L - \dfrac{TL}{3}$

Also, it is given that the thick candle was twice as long as the thin one when he finally went to sleep.

Now, according to the question,

$$\left(L - \frac{TL}{6}\right) = 2\left(L - \frac{TL}{3}\right)$$

$\Rightarrow \qquad (6L - TL)/6 = 2(3L - TL)/3$

$\Rightarrow \qquad L(6 - T)/6 = 2L(3 - T)/3$

$\Rightarrow \qquad L(6 - T) = 4L(3 - T)$

$\Rightarrow \qquad 6 - T = 12 - 4T \qquad\qquad$ [L is cancelled as $L \neq 0$]

$\Rightarrow \qquad 3T = 6$

$\therefore \qquad T = 2$

Hence, Ken read for 2 h in candle light.

32. Going by the puzzled formed by the architect, we get the following form of cubical shape where

Picture 1 is opposite to picture 4.

Picture 2 is opposite to picture 6.

Picture 3 is opposite to picture 5.

Now, working on finding the colour,

we get

  (1) Picture 1 is in orange colour and opposite face of orange is black, so picture 4 is in black colour.

  (2) Now, colour pink is adjacent to colour orange to its left and colour grey is adjacent to colour orange to its right.

So, pink and orange colour images are opposite to each other.

Now, picture 3 has pink colour, so picture 5 is in grey colour.

Also, picture 2 is coloured white and the picture opposite to it is coloured blue.

$\therefore$ Picture 6 is coloured blue.

Hence, the cubical model formed by the architect will have the following details.

Picture 1 (orange) $\longleftrightarrow$ Picture 4 (black)

Picture 2 (white) $\longleftrightarrow$ Picture 6 (blue)

Picture 3 (Pink) $\longleftrightarrow$ Picture 5 (grey)

The adjacent walls to grey colour wall are orange, black, white and blue colour walls.

33. According to the information,

The number of teams = 2 (i.e. orange team and blue team)

The number of players = 6 (i.e. Joginder, Kulvinder, Ravinder, Sukhvinder, Arvinder and Mahinder)

Now, based on performance of preliminary round, team selection is subject to the following conditions

  (i) Joginder cannot be in the same team as Kulvinder.

  (ii) Ravinder cannot be in the same team as Sukhvinder.

(iii) If Arvinder is in the orange team, Ravinder if selected must be in the blue team.

(iv) If Mahinder is in the orange team, Kulvinder must be selected for the blue team.

So, on the basis of above conditions, there are two cases of team selection.

Case-I

Orange team	Blue team
Joginder	
Sukhvinder	
Arvinder	Ravinder
Mahinder	Kulvinder

In this case, four people in orange team which is not possible. So, we have Case-II as shown below:

Case-II

Orange team	Blue team
Mahinder	Kulvinder
Joginder	Arvinder
Ravinder	Sukhvinder

Therefore, as Mahinder is in the orange team, then Joginder and Ravinder will be selected in orange team.

34. Consider any one town, it is to be connected with 3 direct lines with 2 towns, which are in the same zone and 1 direct line with each of the other 9 towns, which are outside its zone. It totally needs $6 + 9 = 15$ and there are 12 towns. Hence, the total direct points to be attached will be $15 \times 12 = 180$, but every line will be attached to 2 points. Thus, the telephone lines needed are $180 / 2 = 90$.

35. In the first row of grids, from left to right symbol @ moves 1 place clockwise in the central 4 squares, * moves 2 places anticlockwise around outside of the square, while symbol Δ moves 2 places clockwise around outside of the square. Same pattern is follow in the 2nd row of the grids and third row of the grids.

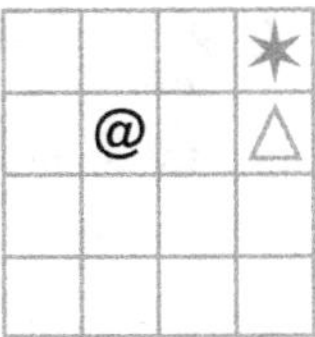

Thus, the third figure of third row will be like this.

Hence, option (c) is correct.

36. On checking every machine carefully, the machine in figure (a) was sorted to have that part implanted in it as shown below.

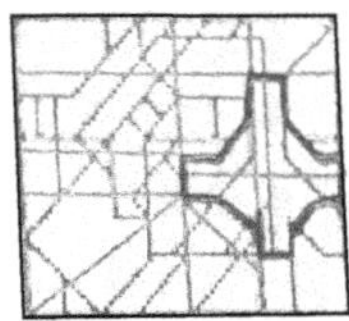

37. As,

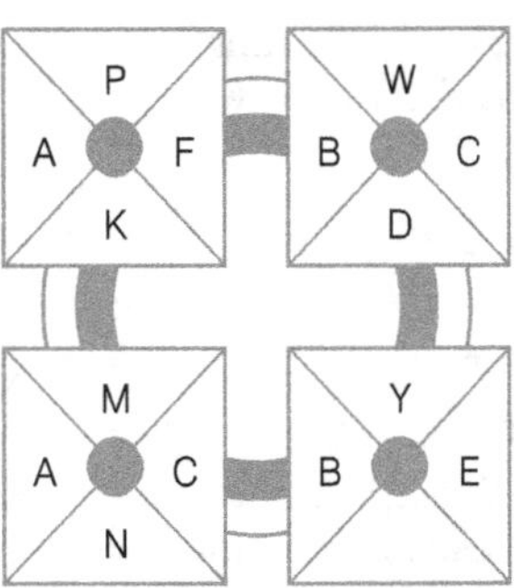

In the first square, combining the positional values of left and right letters give the positional value of top letter and the positional value of top letter is same as the reverse positional value of bottom letter as shown below.

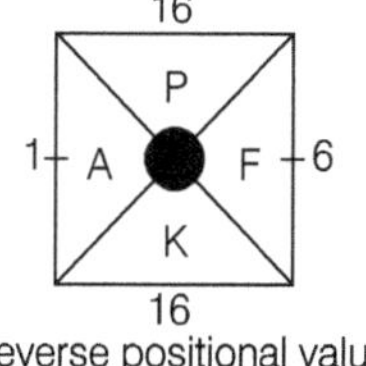

(reverse positional value)

Same pattern is being followed in other three squares.

So, the required letter in the square will be *B*.

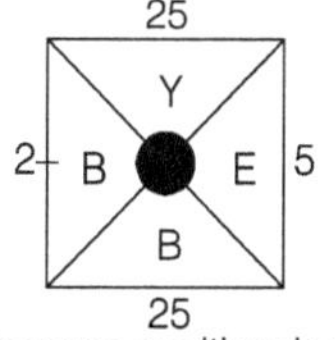

(reverse positional value)

38. The pattern is as under

In the first step, the words are arranged in the order 5th, 1st, 6th, 2nd, 7th, 3rd, 8th, 4th.

In the second step, the words in previous code are arranged in the order 4th, 5th, 3rd, 6th, 2nd, 7th, 1st, 8th.

To solve the problems more easily, we can give numbers to each word.

Input	See	The	Little	Squirrels	Jumping	Here	And	There
	(1)	(2)	(3)	(4)	(5)	(6)	(7)	(8)
Batch I	Jumping	See	Here	The	And	Little	There	Squirrels
(10 am to 11 am)	(5)	(1)	(6)	(2)	(7)	(3)	(8)	(4)
Batch II	The	And	Here	Little	See	There	Jumping	Squirrels
(11 am to 12 noon)	(2)	(7)	(6)	(3)	(1)	(8)	(5)	(4)
Batch III	See	The	There	And	Jumping	Here	Squirrels	Little
(12 noon to 1 pm)	(1)	(2)	(8)	(7)	(5)	(6)	(4)	(3)
Batch IV	Jumping	There	Here	The	Squirrels	See	Little	And
(1 pm to 2 pm)	(5)	(8)	(6)	(2)	(4)	(1)	(3)	(7)
Rest hour (2 pm to 3 pm)								
Batch V	The	And	Squirrels	Jumping	See	There	Little	Here
(3 pm to 4 pm)	(2)	(7)	(4)	(5)	(1)	(8)	(3)	(6)

Passcode for batch at 11.00 am is as "he slowly records to his inner apartment intellect."

Batch II 11 am to 12 noon	He	Slowly	Records	To	His	Inner	Apartment	Intellect
	(2)	(7)	(6)	(3)	(1)	(8)	(5)	(4)
Batch III 12 noon to 1 pm	His	He	Inner	Slowly	Apartment	Records	Intellect	To
	(1)	(2)	(8)	(7)	(5)	(6)	(4)	(3)

So, the required pass code is

"His he inner slowly apartment records intellect to."

39. The answers are 1.C; 2.L; 3.J; 4.B; 5.G; 6 H.

They are highlighted, right on a reproduction of Mr. Alexis's Venn diagram.

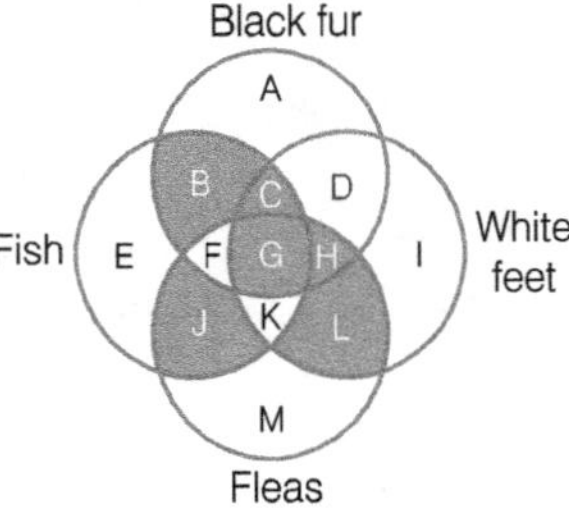

40.

5	?	?	6
–2	–8	–10	?
10	?	?	11
?	–5	–7	2

The pattern in the 2nd row is as follows

(first element) $- 2 - 6 = -8$ [second element]

$-8 - 2 = -10$ [third element]

Here, we don't know the 4th element of the 2nd row.

So, we go to row IV, the pattern is as

(first element) $? - 6 = -5$ [second element]

$? = 1$ [first element]

$-5 - 2 = -7$ [third element]

$-7 + 9 = 2$ [fourth element]

Thus, to get the fourth element add 9 in the third element of the row.

So, the fourth element of 2nd row is $-10 + 9 = -1$ [fourth element]

In I row,

(first element) $5 - 6 = -1$	[second element]
$-1 - 2 = -3$	[third element]
$-3 + 9 = 6$	[fourth element]

In III row,

(first element) $10 - 6 = 4$	[second element]
$4 - 2 = 2$	[third element]
$2 + 9 = 11$	[fourth element]

So, from the above, the missing section will be

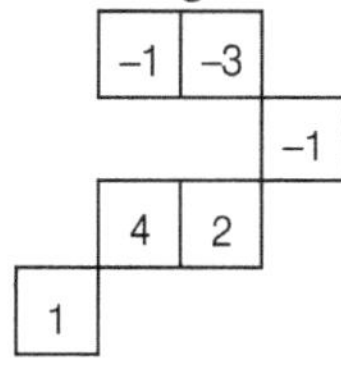

Hence, option (c) is correct.

41. Lets assign a letter to each Goddesses, we get these sentences.

1. *A* says : *B* is truth.

2. *B* says : I am wisdom.

3. *C* says : *B* is lie.

From the 1st sentence, it is clear that *A* is not the truth. 2nd sentence is not said by truth either, so *C* is truth. Thus, the 3rd sentence is true. *B* is lie and *A* is wisdom.

42. As,

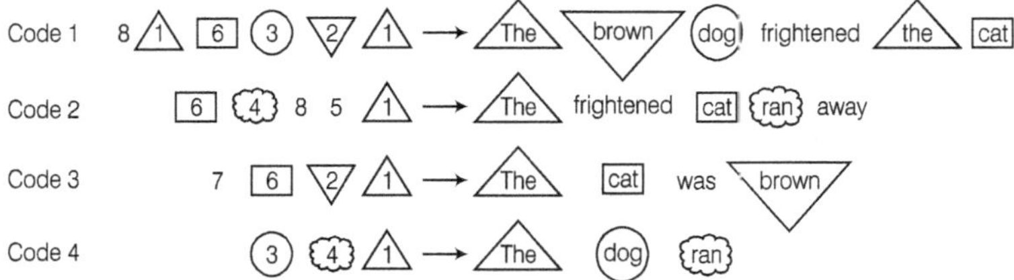

From the above, we get

$$\text{The} \rightarrow 1$$
$$\text{Cat} \rightarrow 6$$
$$\text{Dog} \rightarrow 3$$
$$\text{Was} \rightarrow 7$$
$$\text{Frightened} \rightarrow 8$$

So, the code for 'The Dog Was Frightened' $\rightarrow$ 1378

43. According to the information, the nearest branch of DC (distribution centre) is W_6, which is in South of DC and is 9 km away from DC, as shown below

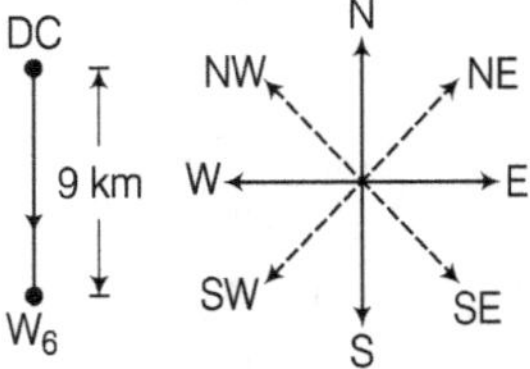

W_2 is 17 km away from DC in the West as shown below.

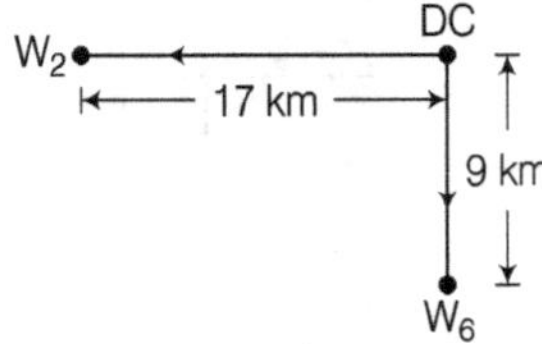

The branch W_1 is 11 km away from W_2 further in West as shown below.

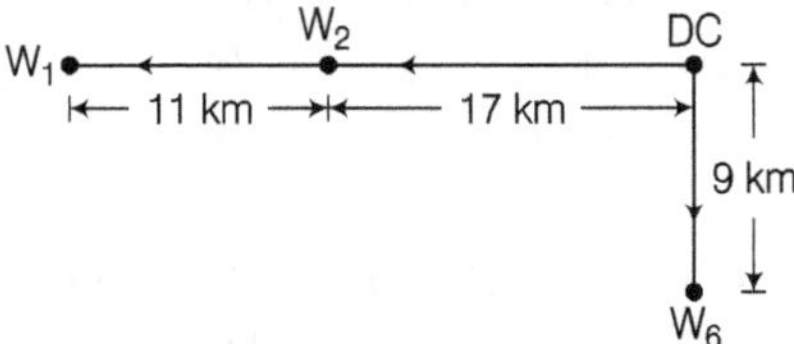

Similarly, according to the information given in the question, we can obtain a direction diagram as shown below.

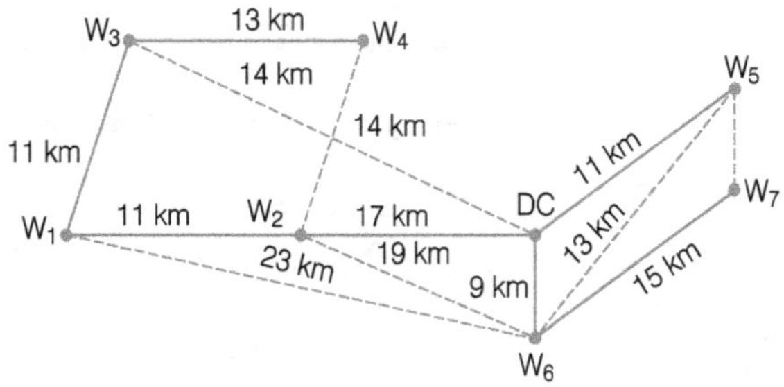

The route that truck has to travel from

$$DC \xrightarrow{14} W_3 \xrightarrow{11} W_1 \xrightarrow{23} W_6 \xrightarrow{15} W_7$$

Total shortest distance $= 14 + 11 + 23 + 15$
$$= 63 \text{ km}$$

44. After analysing the pass codes, it is clear that the words of the previous step are written in the order 3rd, 1st, 6th, 4th, 7th, 5th, 2nd.

According to above pattern, we may arrange the pass codes of each batch.

Batch I 9 am to 10 am (4 pm to 5 pm)	Dig	More	And	You	Will	Find	Water
	(1)	(2)	(3)	(4)	(5)	(6)	(7)
Batch II 10 am to 11 am (5 pm to 6 pm)	And	Dig	Find	You	Water	Will	More
	(3)	(1)	(6)	(4)	(7)	(5)	(2)
Batch III 11 am to 12 noon (6 pm to 7 pm)	Find	And	Will	You	More	Water	Dig
	(6)	(3)	(5)	(4)	(2)	(7)	(1)
Batch IV 12 noon to 1 pm (7 pm to 8 pm)	Will	Find	Water	You	Dig	More	And
	(5)	(6)	(7)	(4)	(1)	(2)	(3)
Batch V 1 pm to 2 pm (8 pm to 9 pm)	Water	Will	More	You	And	Dig	Find
	(7)	(5)	(2)	(4)	(3)	(1)	(6)
Batch VI 2 pm to 3 pm (9 pm to 10 pm)	More	Water	Dig	You	Find	And	Will
	(2)	(7)	(1)	(4)	(6)	(3)	(5)

Now, the given pass code for II batch is "Do not play the near water dirty."

From the rearrangement draft in table we have,

Batch II (10 am to 11 am)	Do	Not	Play	The	Near	Water	Dirty
	(3)	(1)	(6)	(4)	(7)	(5)	(2)
Batch VI (2 pm to 3 pm)	Dirty	Near	Not	The	Play	Do	Water
	(2)	(7)	(1)	(4)	(6)	(3)	(5)

So, the pass code for batch VI (2 pm to 3 pm) is 'Dirty Near Not The Play Do Water.'

45. Three challenges are

$$\boxed{18}\ \boxed{21}\ \boxed{3}\ \boxed{101}\ \boxed{313}\ =\ \boxed{1000} \qquad \text{...(i)}$$

$$\boxed{936}\ \boxed{504}\ \boxed{24}\ \boxed{107}\ \boxed{8}\ =\ \boxed{1000} \qquad \text{...(ii)}$$

$$\boxed{550}\ \boxed{22}\ \boxed{11}\ \boxed{5}\ \boxed{730}\ =\ \boxed{1000} \qquad \text{...(iii)}$$

Putting the mathematical operations $(+, -, \times, \div)$ between the boxes in each equation in such a way that the final result is 1000.

In Eq. (i),

$$18 + 21 \div 3 \times 101 - 313 = 1000$$

Here, we must perform each mathematical operation in the order in which it appears.

$$18 + 21 \div 3 \times 101 - 313$$
$$= 39 \div 3 \times 101 - 313$$
$$= 13 \times 101 - 313$$
$$= 1313 - 313$$
$$= 1000$$

In Eq. (ii),

$$936 - 504 \div 24 + 107 \times 8$$
$$= 432 \div 24 + 107 \times 8$$
$$= 18 + 107 \times 8$$
$$= 125 \times 8$$
$$= 1000$$

In Eq. (iii),

$$550 \div 22 \times 11 - 5 + 730$$
$$= 25 \times 11 - 5 + 730$$
$$= 275 - 5 + 730$$
$$= 270 + 730$$
$$= 1000$$

So, the appropriate order of mathematical operations in each equation are as follows:

$$\boxed{18} + \boxed{21} \div \boxed{3} \times \boxed{101} - \boxed{313} = \boxed{1000}$$

$$\boxed{936} - \boxed{504} \div \boxed{24} + \boxed{107} \times \boxed{8} = \boxed{1000}$$

$$\boxed{550} \div \boxed{22} \times \boxed{11} - \boxed{5} + \boxed{730} = \boxed{1000}$$

46. The smaller wheel turns around 4 times.

Imagine the two wheels turning next to the each other. While bigger wheel turns once (24 teeth) small one turns three times (3×8) to the other side.

Now, we want the big wheel to stop and the small wheel to turn around the big one. There it makes one additional turn on the way around the big wheel. If you can't imagine that you can try with two coins. If you hold one and roll the other around the first one it doesn't turn once but two times.

Still didn't get it? Disassemble some clockwork and try it.

47. According to slogan I,

Is there any respect for women is left in the world. Conclusion II is valid that molestation of women has increased in metropolitan cities.

Now, according to slogan II,

All metros except small have failed to secure women.

From the slogan II, it is clear that the small towns are safer for women. So, conclusion III is valid.

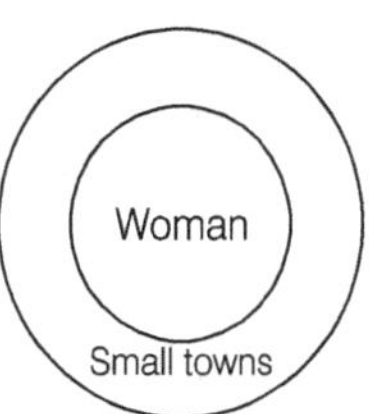

48. Perry's present is in the breadbox. The only truthful note is on the cupboard. If it had been in the fridge, then the cupboard and breadbox notes would both have been truthful. If it had been in the cupboard, then the fridge and breadbox notes would both have been true. If it had been in the oven, then the fridge, oven and breadbox notes would all have been true.

49. As per the given information in puzzle.

Total children of Maan Singh = 8

He has 5 sons namely Arun, Mahi, Rohit, Nitesh and Sourav and 3 daughters namely Tamanna, Kuntala and Janaki.

Sourav is the eldest child and Janaki is the youngest as shown below.

	1	2	3	4	5	6	7	8
Child	Sourav	Mahi	Nitesh	Kuntala	Tamanna	Arun	Rohit	Janaki
Game	Chess	Cricket	Cricket	Chess	—	Football	Hockey	Chess
School	Trinity	Mansarover	Mansarover	Trinity	St. Stephan	St. Stephan	St. Stephan	Trinity

According to the statement, that the 3 sons of Mr. Maan Singh were born first followed by 2 daughters and Kuntala the eldest daughter plays chess.

So, Kuntala will be at position 4.

Rohit was born just before Janaki plays hockey.

So, Rohit will be at position 7.

According to the given statement, that Mahi and Nitesh are cricketers and Mansarover school offers cricket only. So, Mahi and Nitesh will be at position 2 and 3, respectively.

Now, position 6 is vacant, so position 6 holds by Arun who plays football and belongs to St Stephan school.

According to statement, that three of his children are studying at Trinity school and Trinity school offers chess, so Saurav and Janaki will belong to Trinity and play chess.

So, from the arrangement shown in the table, it is clear that Arun is the sixth child of Maan Singh played football and belongs to St Stephan school.

50. As,

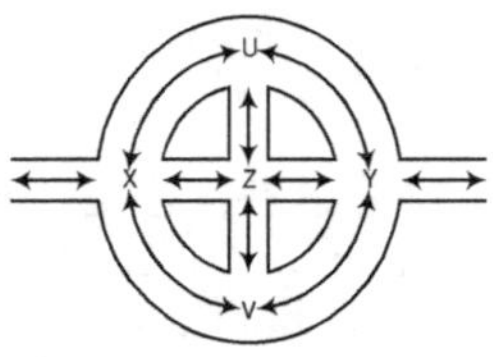

From the above figure, we can determine the maximum number of bus routes possible from X to Y and all routes should be different. The number of routes possible are seven namely,

XUY, XZY, XVY, XUZVY, XVZUY, XZUY and XZVY

51. It is clear from the given arrangement that in the 1st step , the first 3 and last 3 words are written in a reverse order. In the next step, the first 4 and last 3 words are written in a reverse order. The process is repeated to obtain successive output steps.

Same pattern in the password 'Camel road no toy say me not.'

Batch I (9 am to 10 am)	Camel road no toy say me not
Batch II (10 am to 11 am)	No road camel toy not me say
Batch III (11 am to 12 noon)	Toy camel road no say me not
Batch IV (12 noon to 1 pm)	Road camel toy no not me say.

So, the password for IV batch (12 noon to 1 pm) is "Road camel toy no not me say."

52. From board I, S can coded as 03, 10, 22, 34 or 41.

From board II, T can be coded as 56, 68, 75, 87 or 99.

From board I, O can be coded as 01, 13, 20, 32 or 44.

From board II, P can be coded as 59, 66, 78, 85 or 97.

So, any of the combination of these numbers would mean 'STOP'.

53. According to the information, six products (Ariel, Vivel, Rin, Nirma, Gillete gel and Pepsodent) which are to be placed in six display windows of a shop numbered 1–6 from left to right as shown below.

Window	1	2	3	4	5	6
Product						

Rin and Ariel should be displayed next to each other but Ariel should be atleast three windows away from Nirma.

Now, if Nirma is at position 1 or 2, then Ariel should be at position 5 or 6 as shown below.

Window	1	2	3	4	5	6
Product	Nirma			Rin	Ariel	

From the statement, that pepsodent is preferred to be kept between Gillete gel and Rin but away from Vivel atleast by two windows and Vivel can not be displayed next to Rin, then arrangement will be like this,

Window	1	2	3	4	5	6
Product	Nirma	Gillete gel	Pepsodent	Rin	Ariel	Vivel

So, from the above table it is clear that Rin is displayed left to Ariel.

54. Let the colours be red, blue and green. Following the similar pattern farmer's daughter can colour the rangoli with minimum three colours i.e. Red, Blue and Green.

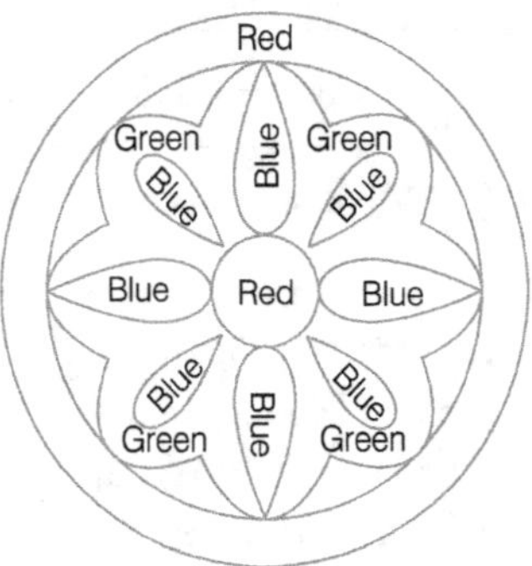

55. When Mr. Maggs replied. "No way, I'm sure" he was not saying that the thing was impossible, but was really giving the actual route by which the problem can be solved. Starting from the star, if you visit the towns in the order, NO WAY, I'M SURE, you will visit every town once, and only once, and end at E. So, both men were correct. This was the little joke of the puzzle, which is not by any means difficult.

So, the route is

$$N \to O \to W \to A \to Y \to I \to M \to S \to U \to R \to E$$

56. Given that, Puneet is from Tamil Nadu.

∴ The 1st statement of Puneet is false.

The 1st statement of Naveen is false and 2nd statement is true.

It is also given that there should be atleast one person whose both statements are true.

That person cannot be Rajni as both the statement of Rajni cannot be true simultaneously.

∴ Velu's both statements are true.

Naveen is from Madhya Pradesh and Rajni is from Andhra Pradesh.

∴ Velu is from Uttar Pradesh.

∴ Puneet's 2nd statement is true.

∴ Both the statements of Rajni are false.

The final table is as follows:

Name	Place	1st Statement	2nd Statement
Puneet	Tamil Nadu	F	T
Velu	Uttar Pradesh	T	T
Navin	Madhya Pradesh	F	T
Rajni	Andhra Pradesh	F	F

From the above table, it is clear that Puneet and Naveen made same number of true statements.

57. The pattern in the rows from left to right, '*' Symbol moves back and forward along the diagonal line, '?' symbol moves 3 square clockwise, the 'O', moves clockwise by 1 then 2, then 3 square etc, and the '#' symbol moves left and right along the second row.

According to the pattern, the third figure of third row will be as,

<table>
<tr><td></td><td></td><td></td><td>?</td></tr>
<tr><td></td><td>#</td><td></td><td></td></tr>
<tr><td></td><td></td><td>★</td><td></td></tr>
<tr><td>O</td><td></td><td></td><td></td></tr>
</table>

Hence, option (e) is correct.

58. It is clear from the table given in question that there are five years and from the statements it is also clear that the years are 1970, 1971, 1972, 1973 and 1974.

Tree					
Person					
Club					
Bird					
Year					

From statements (10), (11), (12), and (13), the table will be like this

Tree	Elm				
Person				Sylvestor	
Club	Squash		Tennis		
Bird				Robin	
Year	1970	1971	1972	1973	1974

Thus, according to the statements except (10), (11), (12) and (13), the final arrangement will be as shown below.

Tree	Elm	Ash	Beech	Lime	Poplar
Person	Bill	Jim	Tony	Sylvester	Desmond
Club	Squash	Golf	Tennis	Bowling	Soccer
Bird	Owl	Blackbird	Crow	Robin	Starling
Year	1970	1971	1972	1973	1974

59. As, the junior carried out the instructions and unfolded the paper to find the code, following shape was revealed through it.

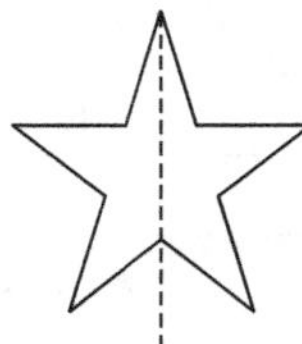

60. It can't be done. Look at this network.

Every time we enter a piece of land we must leave it by a different bridge. So, there must be an even number of bridges attached to each piece of land (except for the start and finish). There are four pieces of land with an odd number of bridges. Even, if we take the start and finish into account there must be another piece of land with an unused bridge. If you remove one of the bridges, then it becomes possible (such a path is called an *Eulerian path*). Does it matter which bridge?

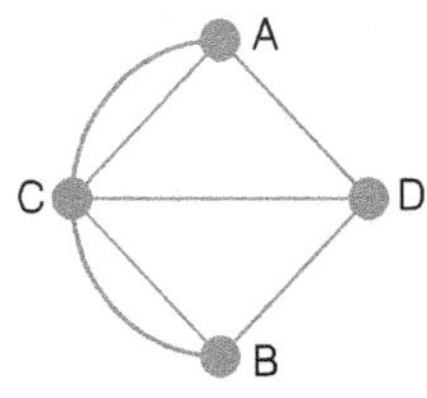

61. We assume that, the radius of the hole in the middle of the wheel is our unit of measurement, i.e. $u = \dfrac{11}{7}$ inches. Then, the radius of the wheel is $11 = 7 \times \dfrac{11}{7}$ inches, i.e. $7u$.

The area of the wheel with a radius of $7u$ and a hole cut out in the centre with the radius u equals $\pi \times 7^2 - \pi \times 1^2 = 48\,\pi(u^2)$. Let's mark by R the new radius of the used wheel expressed in units u when the grinding wheel is handed over to Michael. The area of the wheel with radius R which has an opening of radius 1 cut out in its centre equals half of $48\pi\,(u^2)$, i.e. $\pi(R^2 - 1) = 24\,\pi\,(u^2)$, hence $R^2 = 25\,(u^2)$, i.e. $R = 5u$. So, the diameter of the wheel when it goes to Michael will be equal to $2 \times 5u = 2 \times 5 \times \dfrac{11}{7} = \dfrac{110}{7} = 15\dfrac{5}{7}$ inches.

Hence, the diameter of the grinding wheel will be equal to $15\dfrac{5}{7}$ inches.

62. Below is one of several maximum routes. The shortest route is 1, 10, 11, 12, 13, 9, 27, 28, 31, 32.

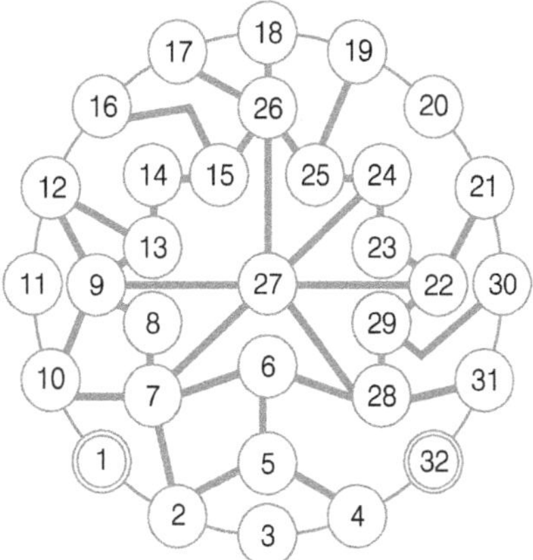

63. Let's think for a while how many exams the student could have passed during his first year-we know that the number must be divisible by 3.

(a) If the first-year student had passed six exams at most, he would in the years to come, be sitting less than six examinations per year, and thus he would have passed fewer than $5 \times 6 = 30$ exams altogether. Therefore, the student must have passed more than six exams during his first year.

(b) If the student had passed at least 12 exams in his first year, then he would in his final year have passed at least $12 \div 3 = 4$ exams. He would then, during his fourth year, have passed at least five exams, during his fourth year, have passed at least five exams, during the third-at least six, and during the second - at least seven. He would have passed at least $12 + 4 + 5 + 6 + 7 = 34$ exams, i.e. the student passed fewer than 12 exams during his first year.

It follows then from subsections (a) and (b) that the student passed nine exams during his first year and three in his final year. What remains then is $33 - 9 - 3 = 21$ exams falling on the second, third and fourth year of his studies. On the other hand, during his second year, the student passed no more than eight exams, during the third-seven at most, and during the fourth year - six at the very most, and thus $8 + 7 + 6 = 21$ altogether, at most. This means that the student must have passed exactly eight, seven, and six exams during his second, third, and fourth year, respectively.

Hence, the student passed 7 exams during his third year.

64. According to the given information,

	Squirrel	Tree	Nuts
1.	Scamper	Oak	10
2.	Tufty	Birch	11
3.	Basil	Ash	12
4.	Gerald	Sycamore	9

Using (3), Scamper can be at 1 or 2. If it is at 2, then from (2), Tufty can be at 3 or 4. He cannot be at 3 because then 10 nuts would be at 2, which contradicts (4), and if Tufty is at 4, then both Tufty and Scamper are correct (invalid), So, Scamper must be at 1 (will the ash at 3). From (1), the sycamore can not be at 2 since this gives both the sycamore and the ash correct (invalid). So, the sycamore must be at 4 (with 12 nuts at 3). Using (2), the 10 nuts cannot be at 2 because of (4), so must be at 1 (with Tufty at 2).

We know that, only Basil can be correct in the Squirrel column at 2 and Gerald must be at 4. The correct tree is the ash at 3, so the birch must be at 2 with the oak at 1. For the number of nuts, only 9 nuts can be correctly positioned at 4, so 11 nuts is at 2.

65. Consider hint 4, if it was false, then it would be true that at least one of the hints is false (most probably hint 4), which would make hint 4 true, and then there is a contradiction. Hence, hint 4 cannot be false, it must be true. Since, it is true, then like it correctly says, at least one of the hints really is false.

Next consider hint 5. If it was false, then its both claims would have to be false, and the first claim is that hint 5 is false, which would make hint 5 true and there would again be a contradiction.

Since, hint 5 cannot be false, so it must be true. Since, it is true, then as it correctly says, either it is false or the hint on the room with the criminal is true but the first alternative is out, since the hint is not false and so it must be case that the hint on the room with the criminal is true. So, four things are known as

(1) Hint 4 is true.

(2) Hint 5 is true.

(3) The hint on the room with the criminal is true.

(4) At least one of the five hints is false.

From (3), it follows that hint 2 must be true, because if it was false, then contrary to what the false hint says, the criminal would be in room 2, hence the hint on room 2, which is the room with the criminal, would be false, which by (3) is not the case. Therefore, hint 2 is true and as it says, the criminal is not in room 2, which makes hint 1 also true. Thus, hints 1, 2, 4 and 5 are all true and since at least one of the hints is false, it must be hint 3. Hence, contrary to what hint 3 says, the criminal is really in room 1. This solves everything.

66. The pattern followed is as under

In the 1st step, the word which comes 1st in the dictionary is placed at the 1st place and the remaining words are written in a reverse order.

In the 2nd step, the word which comes 2nd in the dictionary is placed at the 2nd place and all words except the 1st and the 2nd are written in reverse order. The process continues in the same manner to give passcodes to subsequent batches.

Clearly, batch IV starts at 1 pm. Thus, in the passcode for batch IV, 1st 4 words are arranged in alphabetical order, so as per the pattern, we ought to place the word, which comes 5th in the dictionary at 5th place and then write all the words except the 1st 5, in reverse order, to get passcode for the batch at 3.00 pm i.e. Batch V.

Batch IV Back go here people who settle want to.

Batch V Back go here people settle to want who.

67. (1) All ice-creams are dairy products and all dairy products are food.

(2) Some rockets use liquid fuel, some rockets use solid fuel and the space shuttle uses both liquid and solid fuel.

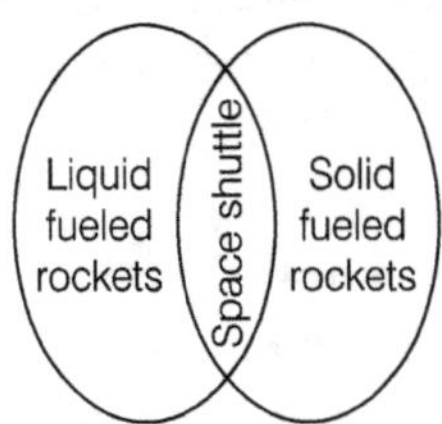

(3) All whales and all dogs have hair. All snakes do not have hair.

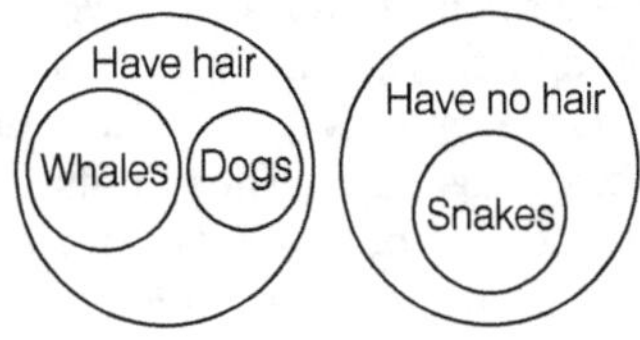

68.

A	B	C	D	E	F
8	25	2	12	20	4

G	H	I	J	K	L	M	N	O	P	Q	R
14	3	7	13	1	19	5	21	24	15	6	18

S	T	U	V	W	X	Y	Z
23	11	16	9	26	17	22	10

Given, T = 11

Consider,

TALK = 39 $\Rightarrow$ ALK = 28

WALK = 54 $\Rightarrow$ W = 26

Now, C = 2, CALL = 48 $\Rightarrow$ ALL = 46

STALL = 80 $\Rightarrow$ S = 80 − 46 − 11 $\Rightarrow$ S = 23

Now, $\quad$ H = C + 1 = 2 + 1 = 3

Now, $\quad$ HAM = 16

$\therefore \quad$ AM = 13

Now, GAME = 47

$\Rightarrow \quad$ GE = 47 − 13 = 34

Also, $\quad$ BEG = 59

$\Rightarrow \quad$ B = 59 − 34 = 25

Consider CHIEF = 36, IF = 11, C = 2 and H = 3

So, $\quad$ E = 36 − 11 − 2 − 3 = 36 − 16

$\quad$ E = 20

$\quad$ F = T − 7 = 11 − 7 = 4

Now, $\quad$ IF = 11

$\quad$ I = 7

WEBSITE = 26 + 20 + 25 + 23 + 7 + 11 + 20 = 132

69. Let's mark the glasses with arrows: ↑ will denote a glass standing stem side up, while ↓ will mean a glass standing stem side down. The initial line-up was as follows: ↑↓↑↓↑.

The first player will win if he/she turns glass 5. It will lead to the following arrangement; ↑↓↑↓↓. Now, the second player has three possible moves: (a) and (b) to turn one of the two ↑ glasses, but then the other player may win instantly, turning the remaining ↑glass.

(c) To turn glasses number 2 and 3, leading to the lineup ↑↑↓↓↓.

Again the first player wins, turning glasses number 1 and 2.

Yes, the person starting the game can always win.

70. According to the given information, we can make an arrangement of boys and girls as shown below.

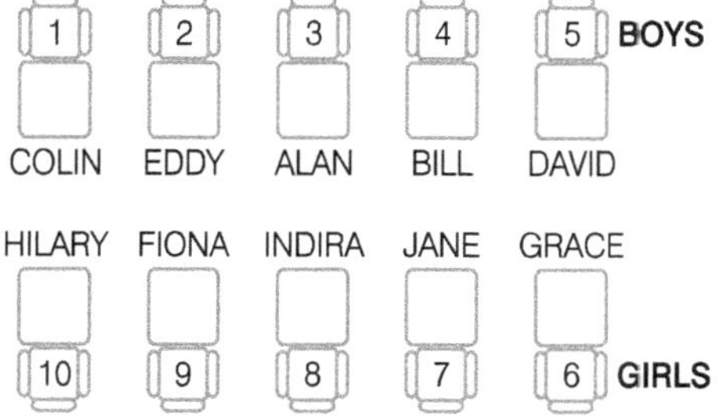

71.

6	2	5	1
3	1	4	7
4	1	9	5
3	1	2	4

Now, player 1 split the matrix vertically into 2 equal halves and choose right half.

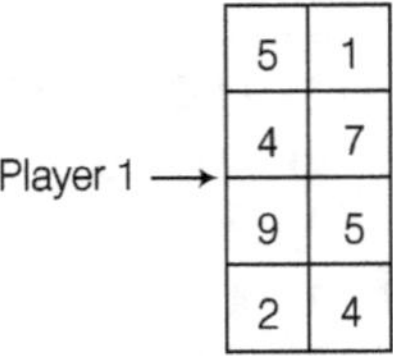

Now, player 2 split it horizontally and choose one half.

Case I.

When player 2 retain lower

9	5
2	4

Player 1 split it vertically and choose right half

5
4

Now, if player 2 split is horizontally, then he can choose lower (4) or upper (5).

Case II.

When player 2 retain upper half

5	1
4	7

Now, player 2 split it vertically and retain right half.

1
7

Now, player (2) split it horizontally and retain upper half (1) to minimise the gain.

72. The consecutive numbers are 9, 10, 11, 12, 13, 14, and 15.

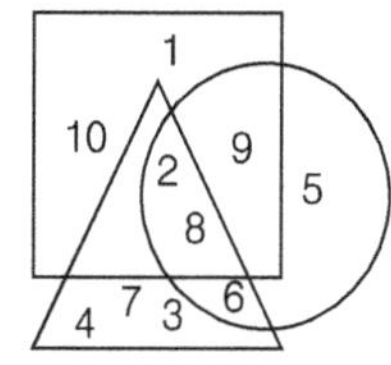

In column I, total of $6 - 2 + 5 = 9$

Similarly, in column IV

the total of $2 + 9 + 1 = 12$

In row I, the total of $6 - 1 + 8 + 2 = 15$

Similarly,

in row III,

the total of $5 + 7 + 0 + 1 = 13$.

73. Since, each child was given the same number of identical cakes, the brothers must have bought the same number of cakes of each kind as well. Three cakes (cream cake + fruit cake + doughnut) cost $1 + \dfrac{1}{2} + \dfrac{1}{3} = \dfrac{11}{6}$ dollars, i.e. Jeremy and Roger bought six sets of three cakes each. Six sets of three cakes can be shared by one, two, three or six kids.

We know for sure, however, that among children were two boys, Jeremy and Roger, which means that in the group were also a minimum of two girls. There were, therefore, at least four kids apart from Jeremy and Roger. So, the group numbered 6 kids.

74. According to the given information, place the remaining numbers.

According to the condition (1), the circle, square and triangle must individually total thirty as shown below

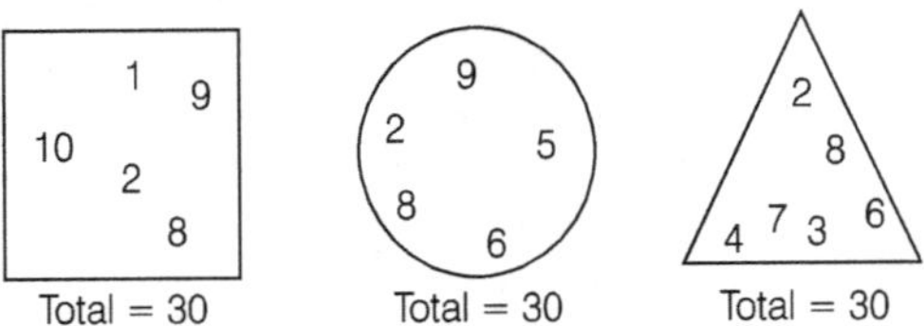

According to the condition (2), the three outer divisions of the circle, square and triangle must also total thirty as shown below

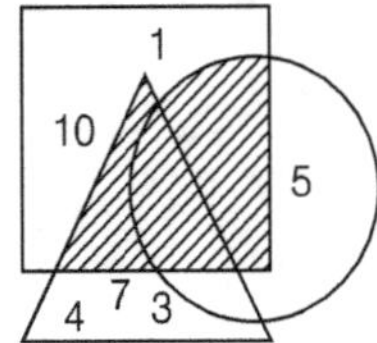

$$\therefore \text{ Total of outer divisions} = 10 + 1 + 5 + 3 + 7 + 4 = 30$$

75. Method I

Group 1		Group 2			
	S	A	M	W	
$\dfrac{1}{3}$					$\dfrac{1}{2}$

It follows from the table that Sophie (S), Adam (A), Michael (M) and Will (W) make up $\dfrac{1}{2} - \dfrac{1}{3} = \dfrac{1}{6}$ of school children in class 5B

i.e. the class numbers $4 \times 6 = 24$ children

Method II

Let's call x the number of school children in the first group. There are $3(x-1)$ children in the class, because after Sophie left group 1 for group 2, in the first group remains 1/3 of the class. We know as well that together with Adam, Michael and will, the first group makes up half of the class, i.e. the number of school children in class 5B is also equal to $2(x+3)$. Therefore, $3(x-1) = 2(x+3)$, hence $x = 9$. The number of children at school is then equal to $3(x-1) = 3 \times 8 = 24$. So, class 5B has 24 children.

76. First, the two sons cross and one returns (because each of their sons weighted 75 lbs). Then, the man (weight of man is 150 lbs) crosses and the other son returns. Then, both sons cross and one returns. Then, the lady crosses and the other son returns. Then, the two sons cross and one of them returns for the dog. Eleven crossings in all.

77. The given information can be represented in the following Venn diagram.

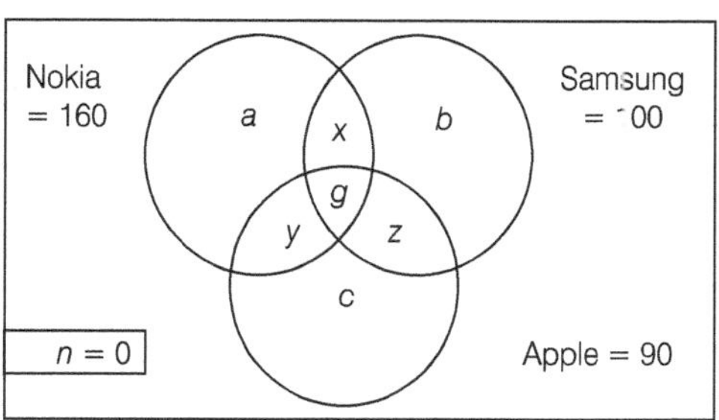

$$N = \text{Nokia}$$
$$S = \text{Samsung}$$
$$A = \text{Apple}$$

From the diagram,
$$N = a + x + y + g = 160$$
$$S = b + x + z + g = 100$$
$$A = y + g + z + c = 90$$

Given, $g = 20$ and $n = 0$

$$(a + b + c) + (x + y + z) + g + n = \mu$$
$$\Rightarrow \quad (a + b + c) + (x + y + z) = \mu - g - n$$

Now, $\quad \mu - g - n = 200 - 20 - 0 = 180$ ...(i)

Similarly, $N + A + S$
$$= (a + b + c) + 2(x + y + z) + 3g$$
$$= 160 + 100 + 90$$

$\therefore \quad (a + b + c) + 2(x + y + z) = 350 - 60 = 290$ ...(ii)

From Eqs. (i) and (ii), we get $x + y + z = 110$

Then, $\quad a + b + c = 70$

$\therefore$ The number of people, who use mobile phones of exactly one company $= a + b + c = 70$

78. Let's define by x the initial number of rabbits. The first customer bought $\left(\dfrac{1}{6}x+1\right)$ bunnies, so the breeder was left with $\left(\dfrac{5}{6}x-1\right)$. The second customer bought $\left[\dfrac{1}{6}\left(\dfrac{5}{6}x-1\right)+2\right]$ rabbits, but we know that he purchased as many bunnies as the previous buyer. Therefore,

$$\dfrac{1}{6}\left(\dfrac{5}{6}x-1\right)+2=\dfrac{1}{6}x+1,\ \text{hence}\ \left(\dfrac{5}{6}x-1\right)+12=x+6,\ \text{i.e.}\ 5=\dfrac{1}{6}x.$$

In the beginning , the breeder must have had 30 rabbits.

Let's check now whether all the customers bought the same number of bunnies.

The first customer bought $\dfrac{1}{6}\times30+1=6$ rabbits,

there remained 24 rabbits.

The second customer bought $\dfrac{1}{6}\times24+2=6$ rabbits,

there remained 18 rabbits.

The third customer bought $\dfrac{1}{6}\times18+3=6$ rabbits,

there remained 12 rabbits.

The fourth customer bought $\dfrac{1}{6}\times12+4=6$ rabbits,

there remained 6 rabbits.

The fifth customer bought $\dfrac{1}{6}\times6+5=6$ rabbits,

there remained 0 rabbit.

We see that, each customer brought the same number of rabbits (six).

Hence, the rabbit breeder had brought to the market 30 rabbits and had 5 customers that day.

79. Saturday's trip wasn't from Eastering (Clue 1), Southford (Clue 3) or Middleham (5), so either Northbrook or Westbury. The trip from Westbury was to Oneford (4). The one from Northbrook wasn't to Twobury (5), so the trip to Twobury wasn't on Saturday. No trips were made on Wednesday (grid), so Tuesday's was from Middleham (5) and Thursday's was to Twobury. Either the fruit was taken on Thursday and the trip to Foursham was on Friday (1), or the fruit was taken on Friday and the trip to Foursham was on Saturday; i.e. Friday's trip involved either fruit or a journey to

Foursham. So, the stationery was taken to Fivewood (4) on either Tuesday or Saturday and the Westbury-Oneford trip was on either Monday or Friday. Thus, Saturday's trip was from Northbrook. Monday's wasn't to Threeton (3), so must be Oneford. The stationery was taken on Tuesday (4). Thursday's trip was from Eastering (1), the fruit was taken on Friday, and the trip to Foursham was on Saturday. Friday's trip was from Southford to Threeton.

Saturday's delivery wasn't of cheese or shoes (2), so must be books. The cheese was taken on Monday (2) and the shoes on Thursday.

Thus,

Day	From	To	Load
Monday	Westbury	Oneford	Cheese
Tuesday	Middleham	Fivewood	Stationery
Thursday	Eastering	Twobury	Shoes
Friday	Southford	Threeton	Fruit
Saturday	Northbrook	Foursham	Books

80. According to the information, we can make a table as shown below:

	Pet	Street 1	Street 2
1.	Dog	Rubble	Lane
2.	Elephant	Hollow	Avenue
3.	Alligator	Purple	Crescent
4.	Parakeet	Apple	Drive
5.	Cat	Grunter	Road
6.	Frog	Tempest	Walk

From (6), Hollow can be at 1 or 2. If it is at 1 (with the frog at 5 and crescent at 2), from (1), Rubble can only fit at 2 (with the alligator at 4 and Drive at 5). Using (2) and (3), Purple can only be at 4 but this means that both the dog and alligator are correct (invalid). So, hollow is not at 1 and must be at 2 (with crescent at 3 and the frog at 6). From (1), Rubble can be at 1 or 3. If it is at 3, both Hollow and Rubble are correct (invalid). So, Rubble is at 1 (with the alligator at 3 and Drive at 4). Using (3) and (4), Avenue can only be at 2 (with Purple at 3 and the dog at 1). For the Pet column, the frog is correct at 6, the parakeet is wrong at 5, cannot be at 2 due to (5) so must be at 4. The cat cannot be at 2 due to (5) so must appear at 5 with the elephant at 2. The Street 1 column has Hollow correct at 2. Tempest is wrong at 4, cannot be at 5 due to (2), so must be at 6. Apple, being wrong at 5, can only be at 4 with Grunter at 5. In the Street 2 column, Crescent is correct at 3. Lane is wrong at 6, cannot be at 5 due to (4), so must be at 1. Walk is wrong at 5 so must be at 6 with Road at 5.

81. According to the given information, we can draw a table.

Subjects \ Students	Anne	Bess	Candice
Physics	✗	✓	✓
Algebra	✓	✗	✓
English	✗	✓	✓
History	✓	✗	✓
French	✓	✓	✗
Japanese	✓	✓	✗

There are three students – Anne, Bess, Candice each study four subjects. Two of them study physics; two study Algebra; two study English; two study History; two study French; two study Japanese.

According to Anne

When she studies Algebra, then she also takes history, if we consider this condition, then she will not take English as per second statement therefore she can also take Japanese. Now, we are left with Physics and French. So, she can take either of it.

According to Bess

If she studies English, then she will also take Japanese, if we take this condition then she will not take Algebra and therefore can take French.

According to Candice

If she studies French, then she does not take Algebra. But Bess does not take Algebra. So, Candice will take Algebra. Given that, if she studies Japanese she does not take English. But Anne and Bess have already taken Japanese. So, Candice will take English.

Now, Candice takes Algebra, so Anne will take French. Also, Physics can be taken by Bess and Candice. Now, Anne and Bess have taken four subjects, so History will be taken by Candice.

82.

	Animal	Name	Prize
1.	Frog	Lorena	Carrot
2.	Badger	Harry	Porsche
3.	Antelope	Ian	Radiator
4.	Dog	George	Microwave
5.	Elephant	Jenny	Television
6.	Cat	Karen	Spoon

According to the condition (4), spoon is three places below Ian and two below dog, then Ian can occupies 1, 2 or 3 position but according to fact (4) spoon is two places below dog. So, according to this. Ian, dog and spoon must be at (3), (6) and (4). respectively. If he is at 1, from (5), Lorena can be at 2 or 4. At position (2), condition (3) is violated and at position 4, from condition (2), Harry can not fit.

- If Ian is at 2, from condition (5), Lorena can only be at 3 but again condition (3) is violated.

- From condition (5), Lorena can be at 1 or 4. At position 4, condition (3) is violated. So, Lorena is at 1, whereas antelope and porsche are at 3 and 2, respectively.

- In the first column, antelope is at correct position, according to condition (5).

- Badger is wrong at position 1 and can not be at position 6 due to the condition (1), so must be at position 2.

- Frog is wrong at position (6), so can only be at position (1), leaving cat at position (6).

- According to the condition (2) Harry, elephant and microwave are correct at positions (2), (5) and (4), respectively. George is wrong at position 5 and can not be at (6) due to condition (1) so must be at (4). Jenny is wrong at 6, so must be at position (5) with Karen at position (6).

- According to the condition (3), since Ian is not carrot, then carrot is not at position (3). Carrot is wrong at 5, so must be at position (1). So, television is wrong at position (3). It must be at position (5) with radiator at position (3).

83. The cards total 84 (Intro), so there is no 7. Thus, card F isn't a 10 (Clue 2). L isn't a 2 (Clue 2). So, the 2 of Spades is either 1 or K (Clue 1) and B, D, E, G, J and L are all Hearts or Diamonds (Intro). The value of card F is 3 higher than that of C (2), so the Ace of Hearts isn't B (3) or D, thus it's E or G. If G is the Ace of Hearts, then E is the 10 of Diamonds (1), I the 2 of Spades, K is a Club, and A is the 6. But then C is a 5 (2), F is an 8, and L is the Jack, leaving no value for B (4). Thus, the Ace of Hearts is E (3), G is the 10 of Diamonds (1 and Intro), K is the 2 of Spades, and C is the 6 of Clubs. F is a 9 (2) and L is a Queen. I is a Club, A is a Spade, H is a Club (3), and F is a Spade. I isn't the Jack (4), so I is the 8 and H is the 5 (3). The Jack of Diamonds is D (4), B is the 4 of Hearts, L is a Heart, and J is a Diamond. The King isn't A (2), so must be J. A is the 3.

Thus,

3S	4H	6C	JD
AH	9S	10D	5C
8C	KD	2S	QH

84. The sequence of shooting each other is as follows:

You	Bill	Kid
(worst shooter)	50% chance of win	Never miss the shot

Case I If 'you' shoots at 'Bill', then 'you' is definitely dead because 'kid' will shoot 'you'.

Case II If 'you' shoots at 'kid', then 'Bill' will shoot at 'you' with 50% chances of winning.

Case III If 'you' shoots in the air, then Bill (who has the next chance) will shoot at kid because 'kid' is the best shooter and on his chance he will definitely shoot 'Bill'.

Now, 'you' and Bill are left and 'you' has a chance of shooting, so 'you' will shoot Bill with $\frac{1}{3}$ chances of winning, hence shooting in the air is the best option.

85. The information given in the question can be represented as follows:

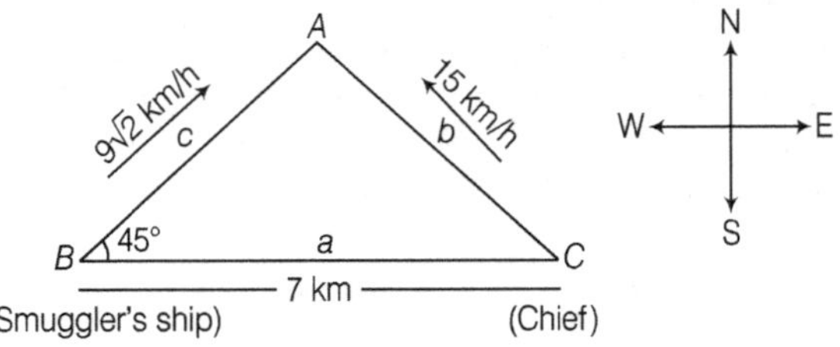

Both the smuggler and chief start sailing simultaneously and stop when they meet, i.e. both ships move for the same amount of time. Let this time be t hours. The speeds of smuggler's ship and the Navy's ship are $9\sqrt{2}$ km/h and 15km/h, respectively.

Using the time speed-distance formula,

we have

Distance $AB = c = 9\sqrt{2}\,t$ km and

Distance $AC = b = 15\,t$ km

Also, in $\triangle ABC$, we have

$$\cos B = \frac{a^2 + c^2 - b^2}{2ac}$$

$\Rightarrow \qquad \cos 45° = \dfrac{7^2 + (9\sqrt{2}t)^2 - (15t)^2}{2 \times 7 \times 9\sqrt{2}t}$

$\Rightarrow \qquad \dfrac{1}{\sqrt{2}} = \dfrac{49 + 162t^2 - 225t^2}{2 \times 7 \times 9\sqrt{2}t}$

$\Rightarrow \qquad 63t^2 + 126t - 49 = 0$

$\Rightarrow \qquad 9t^2 + 18t - 7 = 0$

$\Rightarrow \qquad (3t + 7)(3t - 1) = 0$

$\therefore \qquad t = -\dfrac{7}{3}$

or $\qquad t = \dfrac{1}{3}$

Time cannot be negative, hence $t = \dfrac{1}{3}$ h or 20 min.

86. There are six buildings of different colours red, yellow, white, blue, green and orange in a row. Each of these buildings belongs to different person among Mr. Dubey, Mr. Sharma, Mr. Roy, Mr. Sanyal, Mr. Tiwari and Mr. Reddy.

According to the given information, we can make a table.

	1	2	3	4	5	6
Person						
Building						

Step 1. The green building is three places to the right of Mr. Dubey's building.

So, Mr. Dubey can be at position 1, 2 or 3. If we assume that Mr. Dubey is at position 1, then green building will be at position 4 as shown below:

	1	2	3	4	5	6
Person	Mr. Dubey					
Building				Green		

Step 2. Red building is three places to right of Mr. Sharma's building. So, Mr. Sharma can be at position 2 or 3. If we assume that Mr. Sharma is at position 2, then red building will be at position 5 as shown below:

	1	2	3	4	5	6
Person	Mr. Dubey	Mr. Sharma				
Building				Green	Red	

Step 3. White building is three places to the right of Mr. Reddy's building. So, Mr. Reddy will at position 3 and white building will be at position 6 as shown below:

	1	2	3	4	5	6
Person	Mr. Dubey	Mr. Sharma	Mr. Reedy			
Building				Green	Red	White

Step 4. Mr. Tiwari's building is not adjacent to Roy's building but three places away from Mr. Reddy's building. So, Mr. Tiwari and Roy will be at positions 6 and 4, respectively as shown below:

	1	2	3	4	5	6
Person	Mr. Dubey	Mr. Sharma	Mr. Reedy	Mr. Roy		Mr. Tiwari
Building				Green	Red	White

Step 5. Roy's building is adjacent to orange building. Mr. Sanyal's building is not green. Mr. Sharma's building is not blue, then Mr. Reddy's, Mr. Sharma's, Mr. Dubey's and Mr. Sanyal's building will be orange, yellow, blue and red respectively as shown below:

	1	2	3	4	5	6
Person	Mr. Dubey	Mr. Sharma	Mr. Reddy	Mr. Roy	Mr. Sanyal	Mr. Tiwari
Building	Blue	Yellow	Orange	Green	Red	White

Clearly, from above arrangement we can say that red building is belonged to Mr. Sanyal.

87. According to the given information, the final order is as follows:

Race position	100 m	200 m	400 m	800 m
1	Johnson	Bolt	Powell	Lewis
2	Bolt	Lewis	Johnson	Powell
3	Powell	Johnson	Lewis	Bolt
4	Lewis	Powell	Bolt	Johnson

Clearly, Powell is the first to finish 400 m.

88. We have the following possibilities, according to given statements:

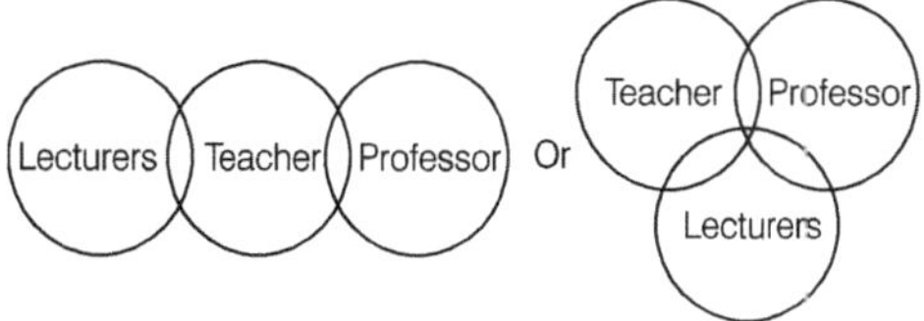

According to the above Venn diagram, only conclusion I is valid. So, possibility I is valid.

89. According to the question, bag can carry not more than 10 books. Some conditions are given about the books in the question and we can make a table by following them.

Book's name	Number of books	Points
Mathematics	1	3
Management	1	4
Fiction	2	2
Physics	2	$(2 + 2) = 4$
Total	6	13

Thus, the total points obtained through these 6 books

$$= 4 + 3 + 2 + 4$$
$$= 13 \text{ points}$$

There is a scope for 4 books. For maximising the points, we need to add 1 book of mathematics and 3 of physics as shown below:

Book's name	Number of book's	Points
Mathematics	1	3
Physics	3	$2 + 2 + 2 = 6$
Total	4	9

So, maximum points $= 13 + 9 = 22$ points

90. According to the information, it is inferred that if the warden Samsher Singh Thapha-visit a cell even number of times, then the cell will be lock at the end. And if he visits a cell odd number of times, then it will be unlocked at the end.

Consider

Cell 1 to 10 ('O' $\to$ Open; C$\to$ Close)

	1	2	3	4	5	6	7	8	9	10
First round	O	O	O	O	O	O	O	O	O	O
Second round		C		C		C		C		C
Third round			C						C	
Fourth round				O				O		
Fifth round					C					

and so on.........

Here, the warden visited the cell 1, for only once and it is open whereas it visited cell 2 and 3 twice so they are closed, and it continues like this. So, the cells with a number having even number of factors will be closed at the end while the cells having odd numbers of factors are open at the end.

We know, only perfect squares have odd number of factors as

$$1 = 1 \times 1 \quad \to \text{Number of factors} = 1$$
$$4 = 1 \times 4 \quad \to \text{Number of factors} = 2$$
$$2 \times 2$$

and so on.

So, all the cell numbers which are perfect square from 1 to 100 i.e. 1, 4, 9, 16, 25, 36, 49, 64, 81, 100 are open at the end. The total number of cells which are open is equal to 10.

91. Given that,

Number of green balls = 7

Number of red balls   = 3

Total number of balls = 7 + 3 = 10

According to the condition (A),

If each ball is replaced before the next draw, then the chance on the first draw

$$= \frac{^{7}C_1}{^{10}C_1} = \frac{\dfrac{7!}{1!(7-1)!}}{\dfrac{10!}{1!(10-1)!}}$$

$$= \frac{\dfrac{7 \times 6!}{1!\,6!}}{\dfrac{10 \times 9!}{1! \times 9!}} = \frac{7}{10}$$

Similarly,

The chance in the second draw $= \dfrac{7}{10}$

The chance in the third draw $= \dfrac{7}{10}$

So, the probability of 3 balls chosen being green is

$$= \frac{7}{10} \times \frac{7}{10} \times \frac{7}{10} = \frac{343}{1000}$$

According to the condition (B),

If the balls are not replaced, then the chance on the first draw

$$= \frac{^{7}C_1}{^{10}C_1} = \frac{7}{10}$$

On the second draw $= \dfrac{^{6}C_1}{^{9}C_1} = \dfrac{6}{9}$

On the third draw $= \dfrac{^{5}C_1}{^{8}C_1} = \dfrac{5}{8}$

So, the probability of 3 balls being pulled in succession

$$= \frac{7}{10} \times \frac{6}{9} \times \frac{5}{8}$$

$$= \frac{210}{720} = \frac{7}{24}$$

92. Steve submitted at least 5 problems—if their number had been no more than 4 entries, it would have meant that the remaining school children submitted 3 problems at most (Steve handed in the most). In such a situation, there would have been no more than $4 + 9 \times 3 = 31$ entries submitted altogether.

It was then possible for Steve to submit exactly 5 problems, because $35 = 1 + 2 + 3 + 6 \times 4 + 5$ (i.e. one pupil submitted one entry, another two, still another three, six school children put forward four problems, and Steve submitted five problems on his own).

Hence, Steve handed at least 5 problems.

93. According to the given information, that 'I' is in the same column as E which is not in the centre, then the possibilities of I and E are as following:

D is in the row below, the row which contains F. So, F will be definitely in first row or second row.

A is in the row below the row which contains B and B is not in the first column. So, B will be in first row or second row and second column or third column, then possibilities of B are as follows:

C is in one of the four corners of squares, then possibilities of C are as follows:

E is in the same row as F. G is in the square above A. F is in the same row as A and in the same column as C. E is in the row below the row which contains B. H is in the same row as I, the same column as F and in a corner square.

144

So, as per the above information, we get the following arrangement:

C	G	B
F	A	E
H	D	I

94.

I.	1	4	–3	–1	?
II.	–3	?	?	–5	?
III.	5	?	1	?	?
IV.	?	?	–5	–3	16
V.	14	17	?	?	?

In the first row, the pattern is as follows:

(First element) $1 + 3 = 4$	[second element]
$4 - 7 = -3$	[third element]
$-3 + 2 = -1$	[fourth element]

We don't know, the 5th element of the I row.

Now, In the IV row,

(second element) $? - 7 = -5$	[third element]
$? = 2$	[second element]
(first element) $? + 3 = 2$	[second element]
$? = -1$	[first element]
$-5 + 2 = -3$	[fourth element]
$-3 + 19 = 16$	[fifth element]

So, the fifth element of I row will be

$-1 + 19 = 18$	[fifth element]

In the II row,

(first element) $-3 + 3 = 0$	[second element]
$0 - 7 = -7$	[third element]
$-7 + 2 = -5$	[fourth element]
$-5 + 19 = 14$	[fifth element]

In the III row,

(first element) $5 + 3 = 8$ [second element]

$8 - 7 = 1$ [third element]

$1 + 2 = 3$ [fourth element]

$3 + 19 = 22$ [fifth element]

In the V row,

(first element) $14 + 3 = 17$ [second element]

$17 - 7 = 10$ [third element]

$10 + 2 = 12$ [fourth element]

$12 + 19 = 31$ [fifth element]

So, from the above, the missing section will be like this,

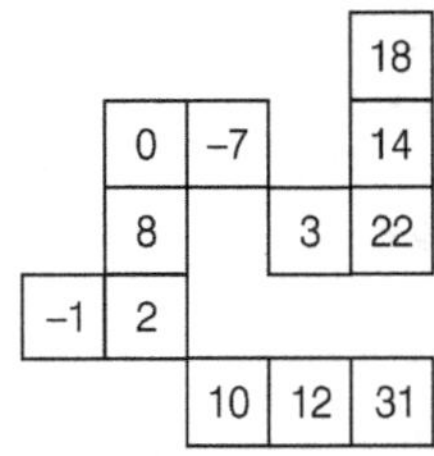

Hence, option (a) is correct.

95. Brutal Ben won and the punches were right jab (Ben), left to the body (Fred), right hook (Fred), left uppercut (Ben), right uppercut (Fred), right to the body (Ben), left jab (Fred), left hook (Ben).

From (1) and (2), the fourth punch in (3) is neither FLJ (Fred's Left Jab) nor FRH. Since, neither BLU nor BRJ are consistent with (3). So, it must be either FRU or FLB. Suppose, the fourth place in (3) is FLB. Then, the first in (3) is either FLJ or FRH; it can't be FRU due to (4). If it is FLJ, then from (1), BLU is three places before the first.

96. Below is a table showing different combinations and probabilities of the dice. From the total combinations, we can see that there are a total of thirty-six chances.

Total Number Showing on Dice	Total Combinations	Chances
2	1	1/36
3	2	2/36
4	3	3/36
5	4	4/36
6	5	5/36
7	6	6/36
8	5	5/36
9	4	4/36
10	3	3/36
11	2	2/36
12	1	1/36

You can see there are three ways to roll a 10 and six ways to roll a 7. Out of these nine possibilities, three are favourable for a win. Therefore, the chances for winning with 10 as a point are one in three.

97. This question can be solved by hit and trial method. Let us take the number of apples to be 79.

$$79 - 1 = 78$$
$$\Rightarrow \quad 78 \div 3 = 26$$

26 apples were taken by 1st boy.

$$78 - 26 = 52 \text{ apples are left.}$$
$$52 - 1 = 51$$
$$\Rightarrow \quad 51 \div 3 = 17$$

17 apples were taken by 2nd boy.

$$51 - 17 = 34 \text{ apples are left.}$$
$$34 - 1 = 33$$
$$\Rightarrow \quad 33 \div 3 = 11$$

11 apples were taken by the 3rd boy.

$$33 - 11 = 22 \text{ apples are left.}$$

$22 - 1 = 21$ which is divisible among 3 in 7 each.

98. According to the information, the cells in this grid contain the digits 1 to 9 in random order.

	A	B	C
1			
2			
3			

Column A contains no odd digits, then column 'A' can contain the numbers 2, 4, 6 or 8.

Possible arrangements are

	A	B	C
1	2		
2	4		
3	6		

	A	B	C
1	6		
2	2		
3	4		

	A	B	C
1	4		
2	2		
3	8		

	A	B	C
1	2		
2	6		
3	4		

If we assume arrangement as shown below:

	A	B	C
1	6		
2	2		
3	4		

From the statement that 'number 7 is in column B, its left hand neighbours is not 4', then B_1 or B_2 can hold the number 7. If we assume that B_2 holds the number 7, then arrangement will be like this,

	A	B	C
1	6		
2	2	7	
3	4		

Now, five numbers are left i.e. 1, 3, 5, 8 and 9. According to the statements, 'cell C_3 – cell $C_2 = 4$ and the sum of the digits in column C is 14, then arrangement will be like as shown below.

	A	B	C
1	6		
2	2	7	1
3	4		5

Now, three numbers are left i.e. 3, 8 and 9, The statements state that the sum of three digits in row 1 is 17 and the sum of the digits in column C is 14, then arrangement will be like as shown below:

	A	B	C
1	6	3	8
2	2	7	1
3	4	9	5

So, it is clear from the arrangement that B_3 cell holds the number 9.

99.

Animal	Breakfast	Place
Cow	Cornflakes	Barn
Goat	Porridge	Field
Horse	Grits	Shed
Pig	Toast	House

According to the facts (5) and (7), pig must eat in the barn or the house. According to the fact (3), if pig eats in the barn, it must eat cornflakes or porridge but in the facts (2) and (7), the animal that eats cornflakes is the horse or the cow and pig does not eat in the field and is not the porridge eater. So, the pig eats in the house.

According to the fact (1), the horse eats in the shed. By the facts (2) and (7), the pig can eat toast or grits, but from fact (6), grits is eliminated. So, the pig eats toast in the house.

Now, according to the facts (4) and (6), the horse must eat the grits in the shed. By the fact (2), the cow eats cornflakes in the barn, so the goat eats porridge in the field.

100.

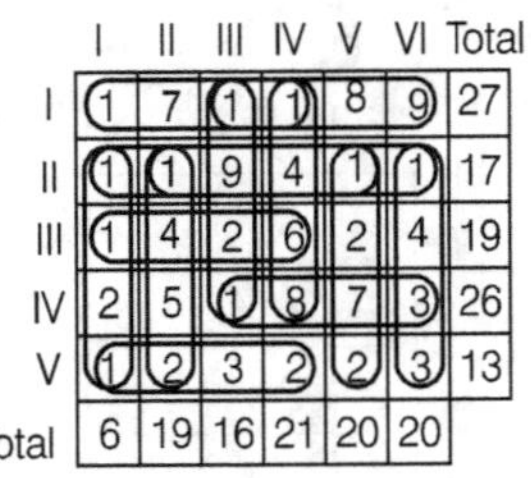

	I	II	III	IV	V	VI	Total
I	1	7	1	1	8	9	27
II	1	1	9	4	1	1	17
III	1	4	2	6	2	4	19
IV	2	5	1	8	7	3	26
V	1	2	3	2	2	3	13
Total	6	19	16	21	20	20	

Year		Place
1121	$\rightarrow$	(In I column)
1189	$\rightarrow$	(In I row)
1194	$\rightarrow$	(In II row)
1232	$\rightarrow$	(In V row)
1272	$\rightarrow$	(In V column)
1426	$\rightarrow$	(In III row)
1433	$\rightarrow$	(In VI column)
1452	$\rightarrow$	(In II column)
1468	$\rightarrow$	(In IV column)
1711	$\rightarrow$	(In I row)
1873	$\rightarrow$	(In IV row)
1921	$\rightarrow$	(In III column)
1941	$\rightarrow$	(In II row)

101. Let the number be a.

Since, the sequence is as follows:

$$a = 2 \bmod 3 \,(3 - 2 = 1)$$
$$a = 4 \bmod 5 \,(5 - 4 = 1)$$
$$a = 6 \bmod 7 \,(7 - 6 = 1)$$
$$a = 8 \bmod 9 \,(9 - 8 = 1)$$

and $\qquad a = 0 \bmod 11$

Now, LCM of (3, 5, 7, 9) $= 315$

Here, $(315 - 1) \times 11 = 314 \times 11 = 3454$

but $3454 = 1 \bmod 3$.

So, it doesn't satisfy the condition.

Also, $315 \times 11 = 3465$

and $3465 - 1 = 3464$ which again is not divisible by 11.

Now, we find the multiple of 315.

315, 630, 945, 1260, 1575, 1890, 2205, 2520, 2835 and so on.

Among all these multiple only 2520 satisfies the condition that $(2520 - 1)$ is divisible by 11.

i.e. $2520 - 1 = 2519 \div 11 = 229$

and $2519 = 2 \bmod 3$

$2519 = 4 \bmod 5$

$2519 = 6 \bmod 7$

$2519 = 8 \bmod 9$

and $2519 = 0 \bmod 11$

Hence, 2519 is the required number. So, the number of prisoners are 2519.

102. The gold was in the bottom left corner square of the map grid.

Green	Yellow	Red	Violet
Brown	Crimson	Purple	Grey
Lavender	Indigo	Orange	Turquoise
Gold	White	Blue	Pink

From (2), (4) and (8), one row has lavender, indigo, orange, consecutively with white one square vertically below the indigo. Using (3), (6) and (9), the purple is one square vertically below the red, the grey is one horizontally to the right of the purple, and the turquoise is one vertically below the grey. From (5) and (10), the brown is one vertically below the green and the crimson is one horizontally to the right of the brown. Together with (1) and (7), these make five jigsaw pieces that can only fit together in a 4 × 4 grid one way. The single vacant square is the gold.

103. There are 4 teams of married couple only.

Score of teams = 2, 4, 6, 8

Team name	Member	Points
Sweet couple	Laxman and Waheda	2
Bindass singing	Sanjeev and Leena	4
Just singing	Tapas and Sania	6
New singing	Mukesh and Divya	8

Tapas and Sania → Married couple → Same team (not sweet couple)

Score of 'Bindass singing' = Score of Laxman's team + 2

'Just singing' team's score = 6 point

Waheda is not the member of 'new singing'.

$\therefore$ Score of Mukesh's team = 4 + 4 = 8

= New singing

By above all statements, we can easily find the each member's group and score. Table shown above is all about the singing competition.

$\therefore$ Laxman's teammate is Waheda and team is 'sweet couple'.

104. According to the information, we can make the table is as following.

Student	Lodging	Studying	Bicycle
Derek	Wheel way	Languages	Orange
George	Saddle Street	History	Red
Hannah	Handlebar Hill	Computing	Green
Jimmy	Bell Boulevard	Engineering	Silver
Sharon	Chain close	Psychology	Purple

From clue (1) and (4), the history student lives in Saddle Street and Computing student in Handlebar Hill. From the clue (3), it is clear that Jimmy is studying Engineering and the student in wheel way is not studying Engineering or Psychology, so must be studying languages and Jimmy lives in Bell Boulevard. Sharon is studying Psychology. From clue (2), Derek does not study History or Computing, so must be the student in wheel way who is studying languages.

From clue (1), Hannah doesn't live in Saddle Street, so must live in Handlebar Hill. Therefore, George lives in Saddle Street. From clue (2), Derek has an orange bicycle. From clue (1), the Silver bicycle is not George's, Hannah's or Sharon's (from clue 4), so must be Jimmy's. From clue (3), Sharon bicycle is not red or green, so must be purple. From clue (1), George's bicycle is not green, so must be red. Hannah's bicycle is green.

105. There were 24 pheasants at the start. Of these 16 were shot dead, 1 was wounded in the wing, and 7 got away but "how many still remained "?" Now, the poor bird that was wounded in the wing, though unable to fly, was very active in us painful struggles to run away. The answer is therefore, that the 16 birds that were shot dead, still remained" or remained still.

106. Carrie had the rent. Denzil occupied front left, Barbara front right, Arnie back left and Carrie back right. Take the first letters of the names and let the order denote the room positions from left to right starting at the front (e.g. BCAD means B front left, C front right, A back left, D back right). Now, if exactly two statements are true, then the correct arrangement must have two and only two statements that refer to the same room (and those two statements are the true ones). Suppose, A is fixed. Then, we can have (a) ACDB or (b) ADBC. In (a), A, B and D's statements refer to the same room, which is too many. In (b), no statement refers to the same room. Suppose, C is fixed. Then, we can have BDCA or DACB. In both cases, no statement refers to the same room. Suppose, D is fixed. Then, we can have CABD or BCAD. Again, in both cases no statements refer to the same room. If B is fixed, then we have (a) CBDA or (b), DBAC. In (a), no two statements refer to the same room, but in (b), A and D both refer to the back right room, which is Carrie's and so theirs must be the true statements and DBAC the correct arrangement.

107. Tanmay is a culprit. He was the only boy about whom just one truthful statement was made by David. Had any other of the 4 boys been the guilty one and the same statements been made, more than one boy would have been telling the truth. But only one boy was telling the truth as stated by Bhanu uncle.

108. From the given information,

			Of only C type foods is 3			Of only V type foods is 2
	Case 1	Case 2	Case 3	Case 4	Case 5	Case 6
Only P	1	2	3	1	2	1
Only C	1	2	3	1	2	1
Only V	8	6	4	5	3	2
PC (but not V)	1	1	1	2	2	3
PV (but not C)	3	3	3	4	4	5
CV (but not P)	5	5	5	6	6	7
CPV	1	1	1	1	1	1
Possible number of V type food items	17	15	13	16	14	15

From the above table, it is clear that based on their preferences, Samara should take 5 CV and 2 only C type foods and Ramesh would take 5 CV type and 2 only V type foods. They would have 5 common foods.

109. There are five contractors referred to the symbols, C_1, C_2, C_3, C_4 and C_5.

The points between different stages of project are referred to the symbols P_1, P_2, P_3, P_4 and P_5.

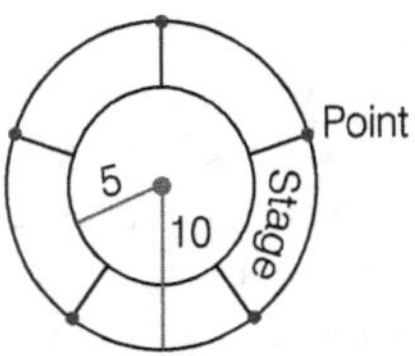

From the statement (3),
Contractor C_5 was given the work of modernising stage starting at point P_4.

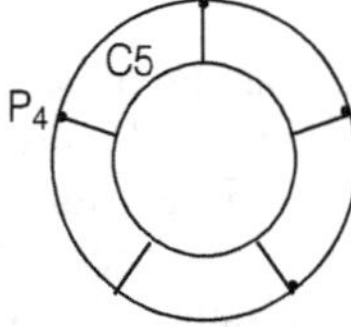

According to the statement (4),
The stage from point P_5 to point P_3 was not the 1st stage.

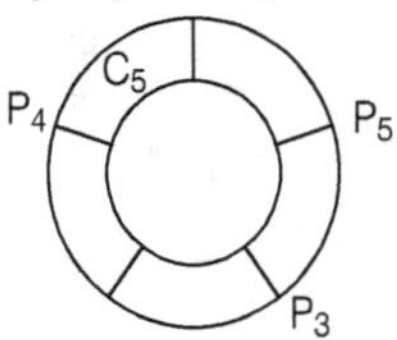

Now, according to the information given in the statements, the following diagram is obtained.

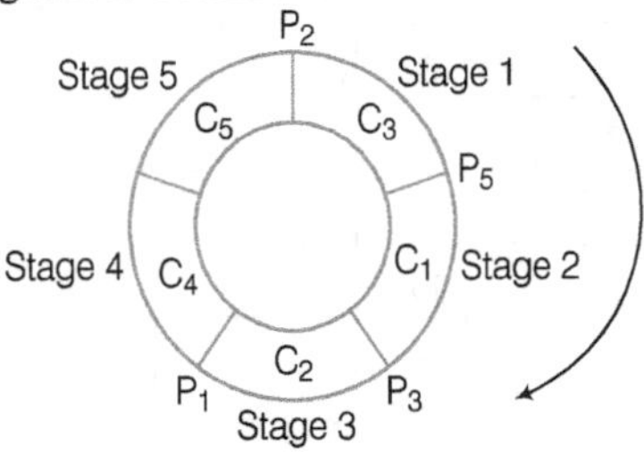

So, starting and finishing points for stage 2 are P_5 and P_3, respectively.

110. According to the fold out of a standard die, the position of the missing pips on the seven standard dice is as follows:

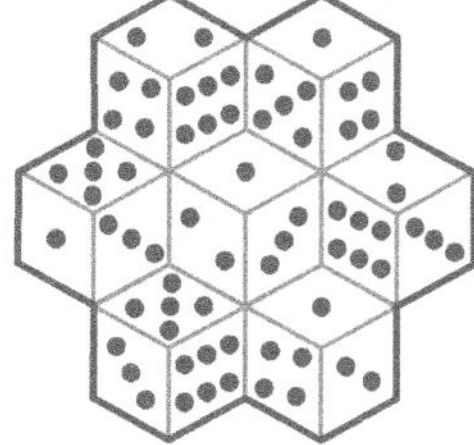
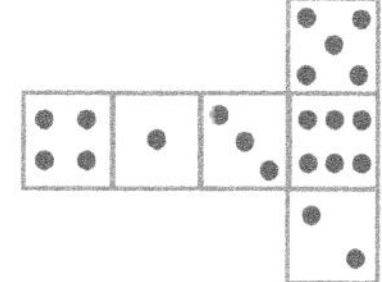

Fold out of a standard die

111. According to the information, we can make a table which shows the balls and their colours.

Balls	Colour
1 and 9	Yellow
2 and 10	Blue
3 and 11	Red
4 and 12	Purple
5 and 13	Orange
6 and 14	Green
7 and 15	Maroon
8	Black

There are 3 players, each player has a different number of balls.

No player has two balls of consecutive number. No player has two balls of identical colour.

The most important point of the game is that it has a winner but the total point scores are as close as possible.

According to the above information, the distribution of balls is as follows:

	Player I	Player II	Player III
	2 (Blue)	1 (Yellow)	
	4 (Purple)	3 (Red)	
	9 (Yellow)	5 (Orange)	6 (Green)
	11 (Red)	7 (Maroon)	8 (Black)
	13 (Orange)	10 (Blue)	12 (Purple)
		14 (Green)	15 (Maroon)
Total	39	40	41

112. The number of handshakes and kisses add upto 55. Each member of Indian delegation said goodbye to each member of American delegation. If we multiply the number of members of both delegation, then the result should be 55.

There are two possibilities.

   I. $55 = 11 \times 5$ (one delegation with 11 members and other one with 5)

  II. $55 = 55 \times 1$ (which is not possible, since delegation is not formed by one person)

We now analyse the handshakes following the same procedure.

   I. $21 = 7 \times 3$ (7 members in one delegation and 3 in other)

  II. $21 = 21 \times 1$ (which is not possible, because none of these delegations has so many members as seen above)

Therefore, one delegation is formed by 7 men and 4 women and other by 3 men and 2 women.

$\therefore$ The number of men $= 7 + 3 = 10$

The number of women $= 4 + 2 = 6$

113. The arrangement of dwarfs,

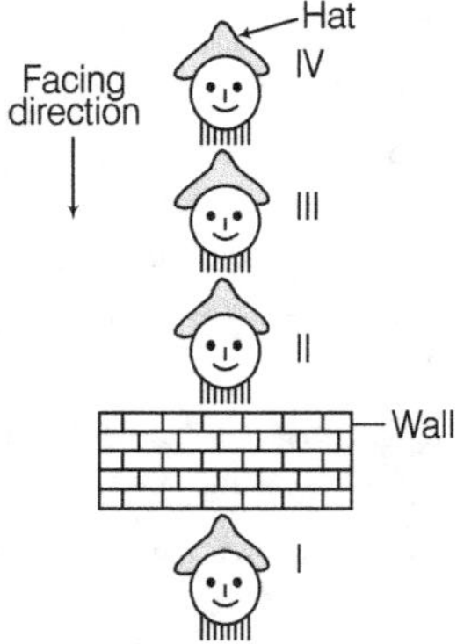

From the above arrangement, dwarfs can not move at all and they can look only forward.

If the II and III dwarfs have same hats, then last dwarf IV will say the correct colour. If the II and III dwarfs have different caps, then the last dwarf does not come up with the answer soon but in this case last dwarf will tell to III dwarf that II and III dwarfs have different caps (red and blue), then III dwarf will simply say the different colour than he sees on head in front of him. Of course he gives enough time to the last dwarf to talk in case he knew.

114. On the basis of the given information, we can make the table as shown below:

Order from top	Publishers	Edition	Subjects
1.	Princeton	2nd	History, Science or Mental Ability
2.	Johnson	2nd	Science, History, Polity or Mental Ability
3.	Holyfaith	1st	Science, Polity and Mental Ability
4.	Reprographics	1st	Geography, Polity and Mental Ability
5.	Penguin	2nd	Geography, History and Mental Ability

Clearly, books on Polity are from Reprographics Johnson and Holyfaith.

115. Let A for Joyallukas, B for Emperor, C for H Samuel and D for Park Jewellers denote the amounts with these individuals, respectively.

According to the information,

The total amount of money with Joyallukas and Emperor together is equal to the total amount of money with H Samuel and Park together.

$$\therefore \qquad A + B = C + D \qquad \qquad ...(i)$$

Now, total amount of money with Emperor and Park together is more than the amount of money with Joyallukas and H Samuel together.

$$\therefore \qquad B + D > A + C \qquad \qquad ...(ii)$$

The amount of money with Joyallukas is more than Emperor

$$\therefore \qquad A > B \qquad \qquad ...(iii)$$

From Eqs. (ii) and (iii), we get

$$B + D > A + C \text{ and } A > B$$
$$\Rightarrow \qquad B + D > A + C > B + C$$
$$\Rightarrow \qquad B + D > B + C \Rightarrow D > C \qquad ...(iv)$$

From Eqs. (i), (iii) and (iv), we get

$$A + B = C + D, A > B \text{ and } D > C$$
$$2B < A + B = C + D < 2C$$
$$2B < 2C \Rightarrow C > B$$

Now, $\quad A > B, C > B, D > C \quad \Rightarrow \quad A > B, D > C > B$

Thus, A, D and C have more amount of money than B.

Hence, B is the emperor Jeweller has least amount of money.

116. Here, when we combine the figure shown as 1, 2, 3 to respective figure (A, B, C), we get the resultant figure 1A, 2A, 3A, ... like this

Here, $1 + A \rightarrow 1A$

$\quad\quad 2 + B \rightarrow 2B$

$\quad\quad 3 + C \rightarrow 3C$

But the figure 2A should have complete black dot which is partial in figure 2A.

So, 2A is wrong.

117. According to the requirements (1) and (2).

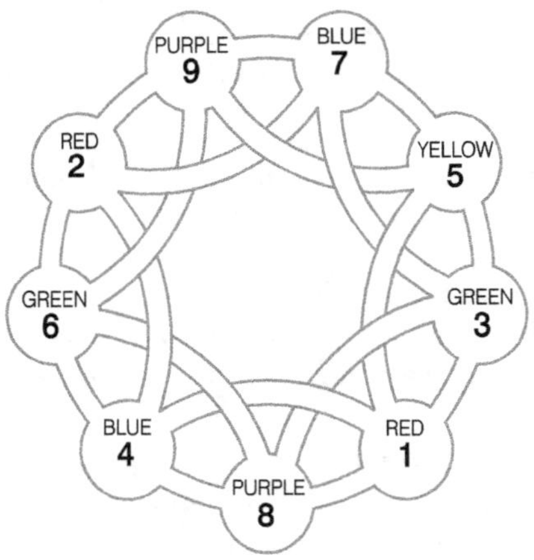

118.

	Male	**Female**	**Location**	**Action**
1.	Henry	Polly	Lake	Sneezed
2.	Quentin	Coriander	Field	Argued
3.	Spike	Bonny	Bridge	Danced
4.	Butch	Tania	River	Cried
5.	Norman	Sylvia	Shop	Laughed
6.	Monty	Daisy	Cinema	Whistled

From (6), Polly can be at 1, 2 or 3. If she is at 3 (with argued at 4 and river at 6), then from (3), Coriander can be at 1 or 2. Suppose, Coriander is at 1 (with Spike at 2 and Shop at 4). Then, from (6), Norman can be at 4 or 5. However, if he is at 4, then from (2), Monty cannot fit, and Norman at 5 gives both Spike and Norman correct. Suppose, Coriander is at 2 (with spike at 3 and shop at 5).

From (5), Norman can be at 4 or 5. If Norman is at 4, then from (2), Monty cannot fit, and if Norman is at 5 (with whistled at 6), then both argued and whistled are correct. We conclude that Polly is not at 3. Suppose, Polly is at 2 (argued at 3 and river at 5), then from (3), Coriander is at 1 or 3. If she is at 1 (with shop at 4), both Shop and River are correct. If Coriander is at 3 (with spike at 4), then from (6), Norman can be at 3 or 5, but in neither case can (4) be true. This means that Polly is not at 2 and can only be at 1 (with argued at 2 and river at 4). From (3), Coriander can be at 2 or 3.

If she is at 3, both Polly and Coriander are correct, so Coriander is at 2 (with spike at 3 and shop at 5.) From (6), Norman can be at 4 or 5 but 4 contradicts (4), so Norman is at 5 (with bridge at 3 and whistled at 6). From (1), Quentin is at 2 or 4. At 4, he and Norman are both correct, so Quentin is at 2 and Bonny at 3. From (2), Monty can only be at 6 with Tania at 4 and laughed at 5. So, in the male column, Butch is wrong at 1, so must be at 4 with Henry at 1. In the female column, Polly is correct at 1, Daisy is wrong at 5, so must be at 6 with Sylvia at 5.

In the location column, from (5), field can only be at 2 with sneezed at 1 (in the action column). So, for location, cinema at 6 is the only one that could be correct with lake at 1. Finally, in the Action column, whistled is correct at 6, so cried must be at 4 with danced at 3.

119.

n	k	a	b	c	d	e	f
1	1	1					
2	1		1				
3	2	2					
4	1			1			
5	3	3					
6	2		2				
7	4	4					
8	1				1		
9	5	5					
10	3		3				
11	6	6					
12	2			2			
13	7	7					
14	4		4				
15	8	8					

16	1					1
17	9	9				
18	5		5			
19	10	10				
20	3		3			
21	11	11				
22	6		6			
23	12	12				
24	2				2	
25	13	13				
26	7		7			
27	14	14				
28	4			4		
29	15	15				
30	8		8			
31	16	16				
32	1					1
33	17	17				
34	9		9			
35	18	18				
36	5			5		
37	19	19				
38	10		10			
39	20	20				
40	3				3	
41	21	21				
42	11		11			
43	22	22				
44	×			6		

Remove every alternating (second) number of this special sequence and check what you are left with (1, 1, 2, 1, 3, 2, 4, 1, 5, 3, 6, 2, 7, 4, 8). Exactly the same sequence which means, if you remove every 2nd term again you will get same sequence again and again. Hence, 'X' will be replaced by 6.

120. There are 16 shelves on a wall which are arranged as shown in the diagram:

<table>
<tr><td>1</td><td>2</td><td>3</td><td>4</td></tr>
<tr><td>5</td><td>6</td><td>7</td><td>8</td></tr>
<tr><td>9</td><td>10</td><td>11</td><td>12</td></tr>
<tr><td>13</td><td>14</td><td>15</td><td>16</td></tr>
</table>

On each shelf, there is a tin of point, each containing a different type of yellow paint. From the statement (1), Amber is below Fallow which is to the left of Cream and Topaz, then arrangement will be like this:

Fallow	Topaz	Cream	—
Amber	—	—	—

Or

Fallow	Cream	Topaz	—
Amber	—	—	—

According to the statement (2), Sulpher is below Buff and to the left of Primrose, then

Buff	—	—	—
Sulpher	—	—	Primrose

According to the statement (3), Cream is below Xanthic which is also to the left of Primrose, then

Xanthic	Primrose	—	—
Cream	—	—	—

According to the statement (4), Lemen and Guilded are to the right of Gold which is below Topaz, then

Fallow	Topaz	—	—
—	Gold	Guilded	Lemon

According to the statement (5), Gamboge is to the left of plain yellow and above Aureate which is to the right of Sulpher, then

—	Gamboge	Plain yellow	—
Sulpher	Aureate	—	—

According to the statement (6), Primrose is to the right of Aureate and below Gilt, then

Buff	Gamboge	Plain yellow	—
Sulpher	Aureate	Xanthic	Primrose
Fallow	Topaz	Cream	—
Amber	Gold	Guilded	—

According to the statement (7), Saffron is above Lemon and below Gilt, then final arrangement is as follows:

1 Buff	2 Gamboge	3 Plain Yellow	4 Gilt
5 Sulpher	6 Aureate	7 Xanthic	8 Primrose
9 Fallow	10 Topaz	11 Cream	12 Saffron
13 Amber	14 Gold	15 Guilded	16 Lemon

121. The gang boss is not standing next to Julian. If this was the case, then Julian would have told a lie only once, while answering question 2 or 3. So, neither John nor Igor can be the gang leader. Julian is not the boss either, if he were, he would have then given four false answers.

Neither James is the gang boss, for if he were, he would not have told a lie even once. Last but not least, Peter cannot be the boss either, because if he were, he would have given false answers to the first three questions. However, if David is not the boss, then among the six captured criminals would not have been their leader, but in that case Julian would given false answers to the last three questions, which is not true. It is clear that David is the boss.

122. By reading the puzzle carefully, we can understand that there are two boys and three girls.

Boys–Henry, Sam

Girls–Victoria, Kathy, Jenny

Now, according to the puzzle, we form the equation to find the ages of the kids.

Let ages are denoted by first letter of their names.

Henry $\to H$

Victoria $\to V$

Sam $\to S$

Kathy $\to K$

Jenny $\to J$

$$H = 2V \qquad \text{...(i)}$$
$$K + V = 2H \qquad \text{...(ii)}$$
$$S + H = 2(V + K) \qquad \text{...(iii)}$$
$$J = 21 \qquad \text{...(iv) [given]}$$

From these equations, we can find the respective ages of the kids.

First for the value of K,

we have, $H = 2V$

put this in equation (ii),

we have,

$$K + V = 2H$$
$$K + V = 2(2V)$$
$$K + V = 4V$$
$$K = 4V - V$$
$$K = 3V \qquad \text{...(v)}$$
$$J + V + K = 2(S + H)$$
$$J + 2H = 2S + 2H \qquad \text{[from Eq. (ii)]}$$

Also, $\qquad K + V = 2H$

As we know the age of J is 21, so

$$21 = 2S$$
$$\Rightarrow \qquad S = \frac{21}{2} \qquad \text{...(vi)}$$

Now, from Eqs. (ii) and (iii), we get

$$S + H = 2(2H)$$
$$S + H = 4H$$
$$S = 3H \qquad \text{...(vii)}$$

Now, put the value of S from Eq. (vi)

H becomes $\dfrac{21}{6} = \dfrac{7}{2}$

$$H = \dfrac{7}{2} \qquad \qquad \text{...(viii)}$$

Now, we have $H = 2V$

$$\dfrac{7}{2} = 2V$$

$$V = \dfrac{7}{4} \qquad \qquad \text{...(ix)}$$

From Eq. (ii), we have

$$K + V = 2H$$
$$K = 2(2V) - V$$
$$K = 3V$$
$$K = 3 \times \dfrac{7}{4} = \dfrac{21}{4} \qquad \qquad \text{...(x)}$$

Thus, solving these equations, we arrive at the ages of all the kids.

$$J = \text{Jenny} = 21 \text{ yr}$$
$$S = \text{Sam} = \dfrac{21}{2} \text{ yr}$$
$$H = \text{Henry} = \dfrac{7}{2} \text{ yr}$$
$$V = \text{Victoria} = \dfrac{7}{4} \text{ yr}$$
$$K = \text{Kathy} = \dfrac{21}{4} \text{ yr}$$

123. Here, the words have been rearranged following two patterns alternately.

Pattern 1 The words of the previous step are arranged in the order-first, last, second, second last, third, third last and so on.

Pattern 2 The words of the previous step are arranged in the order-last, first, second last, second, third last, third and so on.

In such questions, where the terms change places according to a set pattern/order, we prepare a rearrangement draft as shown below:

Input A B C D E F G

Passcode

Batch I (10 am - 11 am) A G B F C E D

Batch II (11 am - 12 noon) D A E G C B F

Batch III (12 noon - 1pm) D F A B E C G

Batch IV (1 pm - 2 pm) G D C F E A B

Rest hour (2 pm - 3 pm)

Batch V (3 pm - 4 pm) G B D A C E F

Batch VI (4 pm - 5 pm) F G E B C D A

We label the words of the given input as per the arrangement draft above and then obtain the desired output for batch V at 3:00 pm.

Input	eight	friends	are	sitting	in	the	circle
	A	B	C	D	E	F	G
Batch V	G	B	D	A	C	E	F
	circle	friends	sitting	eight	are	in	the

124. The cookery book is small (clue 2), so wasn't bought on Saturday (clue 4). Saturday's purchase wasn't the thesaurus (1), atlas (2), the book on trees, or the book on insects (3). Thus, the weather book was bought on Saturday and is large (4), so (1) it's C and the thesaurus was bought two days before book B. The book bought on Friday isn't the thesaurus (above), atlas (2) and isn't on trees or insects (3), so it's the cookery book and the atlas was bought on Wednesday (2). The one bought on Thursday isn't the thesaurus (above) or on insects (3), so must be the book on trees. The atlas is large and was bought two days before the book on cookery (2), thus the atlas isn't B (1), so must be F. The book on insects was bought on either Monday or Tuesday, so isn't B (1). Thus, B is the book on trees (1) and the thesaurus was bought on Tuesday. The insects book was bought on Monday. The cookery book isn't next to the atlas (2), so (3) the cookery book is D and that on insects is E. The thesaurus is book A.

Thus,

Book	Subject	Day
A	Thesaurus	Tuesday
B	Trees	Thursday
C	Weather	Saturday
D	Cookery	Friday
E	Insects	Monday
F	Atlas	Wednesday

125. There are five statements in which nothing is said about the possible offender: A1, A2, A3, B3 and C1.

The statements A1 and C1 seem to be contradictory, but that is not the case! Although at most one of these statements can be true, they can also be both false! For example, suspects A and C might only know each other from primary school.

About the statements A2 and B3, not much can be said (Although is seems unlikely that statement A2 would be false and at the same time statement B3 would be true.)

In addition, it follows from the introduction that statement A3 is true.

On the basis of an assumption about which suspect is the offender, we can count how many of the remaining statements are true.

Statement	A is the offender;	B is the offender;	C is the offender;	D is the offender;	None of the suspects is the offender;
B1	false	false	true	false	false
B2	false	true	true	true	true
C2	true	false	true	true	true
C3	false	false	false	true	false
D1	true	true	false	true	true
D2	true	true	true	false	true
D3	true	false	false	false	false
Total	4 true, 3 false	3 true, 4 false	4 true, 3 false	4 true, 3 false	4 true, 3 false

Combined with the fact that statement A3 is true, this gives.

	A is the offender;	B is the offender;	C is the offender;	D is the offender;	None of the suspects is the offender;
Total	5 true, 3 false	4 true, 4 false	5 true, 3 false	5 true, 3 false	5 true, 3 false

Because it was given that exactly four statements were true, the statements A1, A2, B3 and C1 must be false, and suspect B must be the offender.

126.

What they say they are	Number in the group	What they actually are	What they become
Fibkins	30	30 Switchkins	30 Fibkins
Switchkins	15:15	15 Fibkins	15 Fibkins
		15 Switchkins	15 Switchkins
Truthkins	10:10:10	10 Truthkins	10 Truthkins
		10 Fibkins	10 Fibkins
		10 Switchkins	10 Truthkins

55 Fibkins live in pentagonal houses that night.

Only Switckins can claim to be Fibkins, as it would be a lie to a Truthkin, and the truth to a Fibkin. So, the group which claimed to be Fibkins must be all Switchkins, and so must be the group of 30 x I. The Switchkins of that group thus become Fibkins, because that's what they said they were. Similarly, only Fibkins or Switchkins can claim to be Switchkins, so the group that claimed to be switchkins must be 15 Fibkins and 15 Switchkins and the Switchkins stay as they are. That means that the group that claimed to be Truthkins is made up of all three types-all can claim to be Truthkins. The 10 Switchkins of this group become Truthkins. Therefore, at the end of the day, there are 15 Switchkins (the 15 who told the truth about what they were), 20 Truthkins (10 original Truthkins and 10 former Switchkins), and 55 Fibkins (10 who lied about being Truthkins, 15 who lied about being Switchkins, and the 30 former Switchkins who became Fibkins by claiming that was what they were). Pentagonal houses are used by Fibkins.

127. On following the order of walking on the paths made while not crossing any of the path more than once and not moving diagonally the correct paths that can be followed is

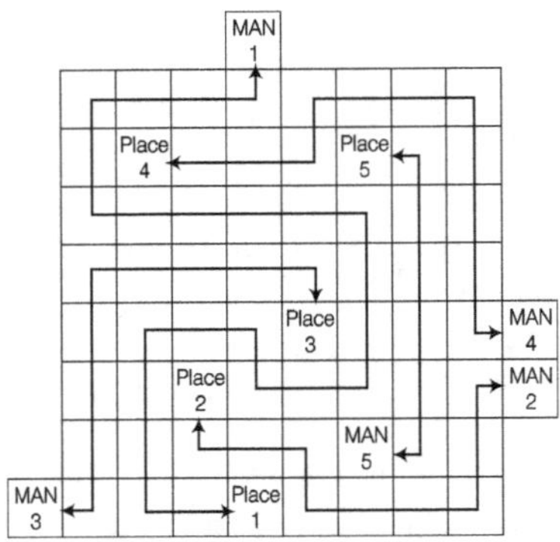

128. The student in seat A hasn't a book on History or Biology (Clue 1), Geography or Art (Clue 6), so must be reading a Chemistry book. His/her surname isn't Brown (2). Nor is Brown in seats B, E (2) or C (5), so he/she must be in D. In clue 1, Brian and Mr/Ms Dart do not have books on History, Biology or Chemistry; so they have books on Art and/or Geography. Thus, Sue's surname isn't Dart (6) nor is her surname Brown (2), Jones (3), or Fisher (6), or it must be Holt. Lousie's surname isn't Fisher (4), Jones, or Brown (5), so it must be Dart. Her book isn't on Art (4), so must be on Geography (above) and Brian's is on Art. Brian isn't surnamed Fisher (4) or (seat D) Brown, so must be Jones. The student in seat A isn't Sue (6) so is surnamed fisher. The surname of the student with the Biology book isn't Brown (5), so must be Holt, and the one surnamed Brown has the History book and isn't Tina (1), so must be Robert. Tina's surname is Fisher. Sue isn't in seats B or E (2). So, must be in C. Brian is thus in E (3) and Lousie has seat B. Thus,

Seat	Name	Surname	Subject
A	Tina	Fisher	Chemistry
B	Lousie	Dart	Geography
C	Sue	Holt	Biology
D	Robert	Brown	History
E	Brian	Jones	Art

129. Let's assume that the number m is the square of the two-digit number x. The number m ends with the digit 5 and we, therefore, conclude that it is an odd number divisible by 5. Since, $m = x \times x$, x must also be an odd number and divisible by 5, which means that it ends with the digit 5.

Thus, $x = 10a + 5$, where a is a single-digit number.

I. We calculate the squares of all two-digit numbers taking form $(10a + 5)$ and check the third digit from the end (antepenultimate) of the numbers obtained:

$15^2 = 225, 25^2 = 625, 35^2 = 1225, 45^2 = 2025, 55^2 = 3025,$

$65^2 = 4225, 75^2 = 5625, 85^2 = 7225$ and $95^2 = 9025$. In each case, the digit is even.

II. We have, $m = (10a + 5)^2 = (10a + 5)(10a + 5)$

$= 10a \times 10a + 50a + 50a + 25 = 100(a^2 + a) + 25$, i.e. the antepenultimate digit of the number m is the same as the last digit of the number $(a^2 + a)$. If a is odd, then the square of a is also odd and thus the number $(a^2 + a)$ is even. If, on the other hand, a is even, then a^2 is also even, so again the number $(a^2 + a)$ is even. This means that the number $(a^2 + a)$ is always even and hence the antepenultimate digit of the m number will also be even.

Hence, the antepenultimate digit of the number m is even.

130. (a) Let's introduce in the table, the remainders after the division of the number $(2a + 1)$ by 7 as a function of the remainder when the number a is divided by 7 :

Remainder after the division of a by 7	Remainder after the division of $(2a + 1)$ by 7
0	1
1	3
2	5
3	0
4	2
5	4
6	6

Let's, for example, check one of the rows in the table. If a yields a remainder of 5 after being divided by 7, then $a = 7k + 5$ for a certain natural k, i.e.

$2a + 1 \Rightarrow 2 \times (7k + 5) + 1 \Rightarrow 14k + 11 \Rightarrow 7 \times (2k + 1) + 4$ gives a remainder of 4 when divided by 7. We check the remaining six rows in the same way.

It follows from the above table that the remainders after division change in subsequent operations according to the following patterns.

$0 \to 1 \to 3 \to 0$, $2 \to 5 \to 4 \to 2$ and $6 \to 6$. This means that if we start with a number whose remainder after division by 7 equals for example 1, then after subsequent operations, we will obtain numbers with remainders equaling : 3, 0, 1, 3, 0, 1, 3, 0, 1, 3, ...

Let's check what number we should start with to obtain after five operations a number divisible by 7 (i.e. with a remainder of 0):

$1 \to 3 \to 0 \to 1 \to 3 \to 0 \to 1 \to 3 \to 0 \to 1 \to 3 \to 0 \to$ ......

If we begin with a number which after division by 7 yields a remainder of 1, then after performing five operations, we will obtain a number divisible by 7.

$$(1 \to 3 \to 0 \to 1 \to 3 \to 0)$$

Here is an example. We begin with 1 and after subsequent operations, we obtain : 3, 7, 15, 31 and 63. The number 63, the result after five operations, is divisible by 7.

(b) After each such operation, we obtain an odd number, so the final result is indivisible by 12.

Hence, the final result can be a number divisible by 7, but cannot be divisible by 12.

131. In the given figure, angle α is marked between the longer sides of the rectangles A and B. Labelling the sides of the inner rectangle B as k and 1 where $k \geq 1$ is the longer side. Now, from the figure given below:

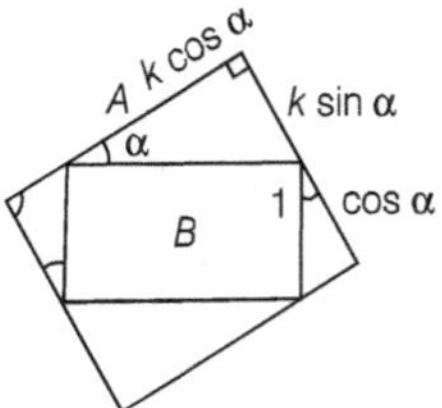

Since, the long side of the outer rectangle A is greater than or equal to its short side, we see that

$$k \cos \alpha + \sin \alpha \geq \cos \alpha + k \sin \alpha$$

$$\sin \alpha - \cos \alpha \geq k(\sin \alpha - \cos \alpha)$$

If it was true that $\alpha > \dfrac{\pi}{4}$, we would have $\sin \alpha > \cos \alpha$, meaning

$\sin \alpha - \cos \alpha > 0$, so that the lost inequality above would hold only, if $k \leq 1$. But, we have assumed that $k \geq 1$. This means $k = 1$, so $\alpha = \dfrac{\pi}{4}$ is

a contradiction.

Thus, $\alpha \le \dfrac{\pi}{4}$.

Now, required ratio of sides of rectangle B

$= \dfrac{k}{1} = k$ and required ratio of sides of rectangle A, because $\alpha \le \dfrac{\pi}{4}$

means $\cos\alpha \ge \sin\alpha$ is $\dfrac{k\cos\alpha + \sin\alpha}{\cos\alpha + k\sin\alpha}$.

Now, $k \ge 1 \Rightarrow k^2 \sin\alpha \ge 1 \cdot \sin\alpha$,

$\therefore$ Ratio of sides of rectangle A

$$= \dfrac{k\cos\alpha + \sin\alpha}{\cos\alpha + k\sin\alpha}$$

$$\le \dfrac{k\cos\alpha + k^2 \sin\alpha}{\cos\alpha + k\sin\alpha}$$

$$= k = \text{the ratio of sides of rectangle } B$$

So, Braden's son followed the magic ratio of his father.

132. The clue for figure 1 is that if one shape is divided in half, all three shapes would be identical, as

Distorted figure	Original figure

The clue for figure 2 is that all three shapes are identical.

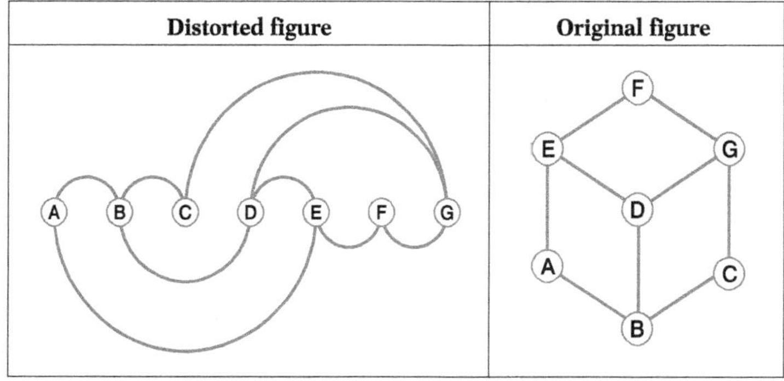

133. From the statement (3), banker will be at position (1) and Fred at position (2). From statement (9), banker catches 6 fish. From the statements (8) and (10), it is clear that Dick is the middle fisherman from Tucson and uses a bait of maggots and two seats away from the man from St. Louis. We assume the position of man from St. Louis is at (5). From statement (4), at the South end of the pier is salesman who catches only one fish. From the statement (6), the man from New York uses shrimps for bait is at position (4). From the statement (11), Dick is a professor and catches 10 fish. From the statement (2), Fred is a electrician and uses bread for his bait. From the statement (5), Fred is from Orlando and catches 15 fish. From the statement (7), Joe is a banker from Los Angeles and uses worms as his bait. From the statements (1) and (12), Henry is a plumber and catches 9 fish.

Now, from the above information, we can make a table.

Gone fishing

NORTH ⟵————————— PIER —————————⟶ SOUTH

Name	Joe	Fred	Dick	Henry	Malcolm
Occupation	Banker	Electrician	Professor	Plumber	Salesman
Town	LA	Orlando	Tucson	New York	St. Louis
Bait	Worms	Bread	Maggots	Shrimps	Meal
Catch	6	15	10	9	1

134.

	Creature	Home	Rise time	Cereal
1.	Frog	Reeds	7 am	Lice Krispies
2.	Otter	Boot	9 am	Pondpops
3.	Newt	Hollow log	10 am	Flyflakes
4.	Toad	Sticks	8 am	Waterbix
5.	Perch	Dam	6 am	Codflakes

From the statements (1) and (6), the Lice Krispies diner can only be at 1 or 2. If it is at 2, using the statements (1) and (7), the Flyflakes diner can only be at 3. This gives two correct in the Cereal column (invalid), so the Lice Krispies diner is at 1 (with the newt at 3). Then, using the statements (4) and (5), the 10 am riser can only be at 3 and so, using (2) and (8), the 9 am riser can only be at (2) with the reeds dweller at 1. Using the statement (7), the Flyflakes eater is then at 2 or 3. If it is at 2 (with the dam resident at 4), that gives both dam and reeds correct in the House column

(invalid), so Flyflakes is not at 2 and must be at 3 with dam at 5.
So, the newt is correctly positioned in the Creature column, reeds
in the House column, 10 am in the Rise time column and Flyflakes
in the Cereal column.

In the Creature column, the perch is wrong at 4, cannot be at 2
due to (5), so must be at 5. The toad is wrong at 2, so must be at 4
leaving the otter at 2. In the House column, sticks is incorrect at 2,
cannot be at 3 due to (1), so must be at 4. The boot is wrong at 3,
so must be at 2 leaving the hollow log at 3. For the Rising time,
6 am is wrong at 1, is not at 4 due to (8), so must be at 5. The 7 am
time is incorrect at 4, so must be at 1. So, 8 am is at 4. The Cereal
column has Pondpops incorrect at 4, it cannot be at 5 due to (3),
so must be at 2. Waterbix is wrong at 5, so is at 4. So, Codflakes is
at 5.

135. Though this problem might strike the novice as being rather
difficult, it is, as a matter of fact, quite easy and is made still easier
by inserting four out of the ten numbers.

First, it will be found that squares that are diametrically opposite
have a common difference. For example, the difference between
the square of 14 and the square of 2, in the diagram, is 192; and
the difference between the square of 16 and the square of 8 is also
192. This must be so in every case. Then, it should be remembered
that the difference between squares of two consecutive numbers is
always twice the smaller number plus 1 and that the difference
between the squares of any two numbers can always be expressed
as the difference of the numbers multiplied by their sum. Thus, the
square of 5(25) less the square of 4(16) equals $(2 \times 4) + 1$ or 9; also,
the square of 7(49) less the square of 3 (9) equals $(7 + 3) \times (7 - 3)$
or 40.

Now, the number 192, referred to above, may be divided into five
different pairs of even factors: 2×96, 4×48, 6×32, 8×24 and
12×16 and these divided by 2 give us, 1×48, 2×24, 3×16, 4×12
and 6×8. The difference and sum respectively of each of these
pairs in turn produce 47, 49; 22, 26; 13, 19; 8, 16; and 2, 14. These
are the required numbers, four of which are already placed. The
six numbers that have to be added may be placed in just six
different ways, one of which is as follows, reading round the circle
clockwise: 16, 2, 49, 22, 19, 8, 14, 47, 26, 13.

	1	**2**	**3**	**4**
Landlord	Colin	Daniel	Bob	Arthur
Guest	Frances	Geraldine	Eunice	Harry
Guest house	Kestrelview	Ivorytowers	Lavender	Jollyjapes

From the conditions (1), (2) and (5), we either have (a) Harry at 1, Bob at 2, and Kestrelview at 4, or (b) Kestrelview at 1, Bob at 3, and Harry at 4. From (2), Ivorytowers must be at 2 or 3, so from (4) and (6) we have either (c) Arthur at 1, Eunice at 2, and Ivorytowers at 3, or (d) Ivorytowers at 2, Eunice at 3 and Arthur at 4. For the combinations (a)(c), (a)(d) and (b)(c), there's nowhere that (3) can fit, so (b)(d) is the correct combination and Frances is at 1, Daniel at 2 and Lavender at 3, which leaves Colin at 1, Geraldine at 2, and Jollyjapes at 4.

137. Let's mark the centres of the circles by O_1, O_2, O_3, O_4 and intersection points of the circle with centre O_1 with circles with centres O_2 and O_4 by A, B, C, D. (See figure)

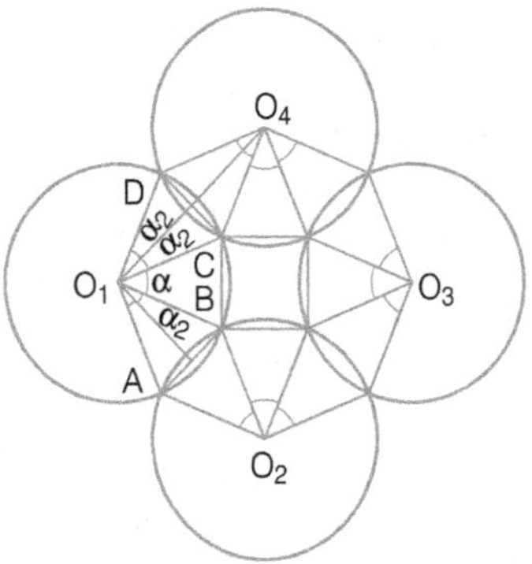

Let's denote by α the magnitude of angle $\angle AO_1B$. Angles $\angle BO_1C$ and $\angle CO_1D$ also have the same α magnitude because they are central angles on the same circle, subtending an arc of the same length (3 inches). Since, the circles are congruent and their shorter arcs are of the same length, all the remaining nine angles marked in the figure also have α magnitude. Quadrilateral O_1AO_2B is a rhombus (the length of each of its sides is equal to the radii of the circles), so its diagonal O_1O_2 divides angle $\angle AO_1B$ into two angles of identical magnitude equal to $\dfrac{\alpha}{2}$. It is just like in the case of rhombus O_4DO_1C and the two remaining ones.

Let's now consider quadrilateral $O_1O_2O_3O_4$. The angle at vertex O_1 has a magnitude equal to $\dfrac{\alpha}{2} + \alpha + \dfrac{\alpha}{2} = 2\alpha$, just as the remaining vertex angles of the quadrilateral. This means that quadrilateral $O_1O_2O_3O_4$ is a square, so $2\alpha = 90°$. Hence, the circumference of each circle equals.

$$3 \times \left(\frac{360°}{\alpha}\right) = 3 \times \left(\frac{360°}{45°}\right) = 3 \times 8 = 24$$

Thus, the circumference of each circle equals 24 inches.

138. The small squares are fit in this way.

E	G	B
C	F	H
A	I	D

g									
e	E			G			B		
c									
d									
j	C			F			H		
a									
f									
h	A			I			D		
i									
b	a	j	i	e	h	c	f	d	g

Now, placing the squares E, G, B, C, F, H, A, I and D into the diagram.

	I	II	III	IV	V	VI	VII	VIII	XI	X
I	g				a	d	b	j	h	e
II	e				i	f	j	d	g	h
III	c				f	e	d	i	j	b
IV	d	e	f	g	h	j	a	b	c	i
V	j	h	i	d	g	b	e	c	a	f
VI	a	d	h	b	j	g	f	e	i	c
VII	f	j	g	e	d	c	i	h	b	a
VIII	h	f	d	c	b	i	g	a	e	j
XI	i	b	e	j	c	a	h	g	f	d
X	b	a	j	i	e	h	c	f	d	g

(1-40)

Now, In row I,

the letter are

g a d b j h e

Given letters are a, b, c, d, e, f, g, h i, j

So, remaining letters are i, c, f

But in column II, f can not fit, so only i can fit in II column.

Similarly, in III and IV column c and f can fit respectively as

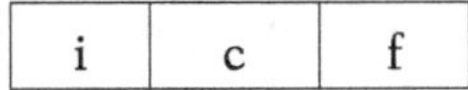

i	c	f

In row II,

the letters are

e, i, f, j, d, g, h

Given letters are a, b, c, d, e, f, g, h, i, j

So, remaining letters are a, b, c

So, c, b and *a* can fit in column II, III and IV respectively as

c	b	a

Similarly, in row III

the letters are c, f, e, d, i, j, b

and given letters are a, b, c, d, e, f, g, h, i, j

So, remaining letters are a, g, h.

∴ g, a and h can fit in column.

II, III and IV respectively as

g	a	h

So, the arrangement of letters is as follows

i	c	f
c	b	a
g	a	h

139. We have to find the unique number which you can get to from the answers to the three questions. There can be only one, or the question would not work.

    1. Is it under 41?

       No 41- 82

       Yes 1 - 40

2. Is it divisible by 4?

Yes	44	48	52	56	60	64	68	72	76	80	(41-82)
No	41	42	43	45	46	47	49	50	51	53	
	54	55	57	58	59	61	62	63	65	66	
	67	69	70	71	73	74	75	77	78	79	
	81	82									
Yes	4	8	12	16	20	24	28	32	36	40	
No	1	2	3	5	6	7	9	10	11	13	
	14	15	17	18	19	21	22	23	25	26	
	27	29	30	31	33	34	35	37	38	39	

3. It is a square number?

Yes 64 – the unique answer

Yes	49	81										(41-82, Div 40K)
No	44	48	52	56	60	68	72	76	80			(41-82, no Div 4)
No	41	42	43	45	46	47	50	51	53			
	54	55	57	58	59	61	62	63	65	66		
	67	69	70	71	73	74	75	77	78	79	82	
Yes	4	16	36									(1-40, Div 40K)
No	8	12	20	24	28	32	40					
Yes	1	9	25									(1-40, no Div 4)
No	2	3	5	6	7	10	11	13				
	14	15	17	18	19	21	22	23				
	26	27	29	30	31	33	34	35	37	38	39	

By answering no to the first question, yes to the second and yes to the third you arrive at the only unique number −64, which is therefore, the number of Archibald's house.

140. Here, is the solution:

G, J and T stand for Giles, Jasper and Timothy; and 8, 5, 3 for £ 800, £ 500 and £ 300, respectively. The two side columns represent the left bank and the right bank, and the middle column the river. Thirteen crossings are necessary and each line shows the position when the boat is in mid-stream during a crossing, the point of the bracket indicating the direction.

It will be found that not only is no person left alone on the land or in the boat with more than his share of the spoil, but that also no two persons are left with more than their joint shares, though this last point was not insisted upon in the conditions.

	...{J 5} ...	...G T 8 3
5...	...(J } ...	...G T 8 3
5...	...{G 3) ...	...J T 8
53...	...(G } ...	...J T 8
53...	...{J T) ...	...G 8
J 5...	...(T 3} ...	...G 8
J 5...	...{G 8) ...	...T 3
G 8...	...(J 5} ...	...T 3
G 8...	...{J T) ...	...53
J T 8...	...(} ...	...53
J T 8...	...{G 3) ...	...5
G T 83...	...(J } ...	...5
G T 83...	...{J 5) ...	

141.

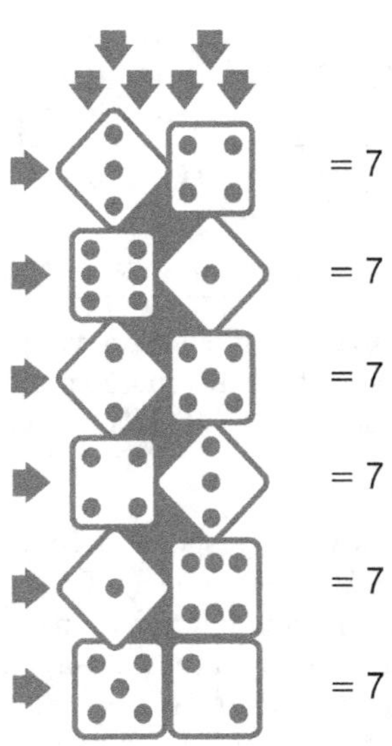

142. Let's represent Bill's cell-phone PIN number by $abcd$. From the conditions stated in the problem, we know that $b = c + d$ and $10a + b + 10c + d = 100$. Substituting $b = c + d$ in the second equation, we obtain $10a + 11c + 2d = 100$. Hence, we see that the digit c is even (otherwise the number $(10a + 11c + 2d)$ would be odd and as such could not equal 100).

Moreover, $11c + 2d = 100 - 10a = 10(10 - 10a)$, whence it follows that $(11c + 2d)$ is divisible by 10. We substituted c with consecutive one-digit even numbers and find d such that $(11c + 2d)$ is divisible by 10:

(a) $c = 0$, then $d = 0$ or $d = 5$;

(b) $c = 2$, then $d = 4$ or $d = 9$;

(c) $c = 4$, then $d = 3$ or $d = 8$;

(d) $c = 6$, then $d = 2$ or $d = 7$;

(e) $c = 8$, then $d = 1$ or $d = 6$;

Solutions in which $c + d \geq 10$ can be rejected straightaway, because it follows from the problem that $c + d = b$ is a one-digit number. We also reject the solution $c = d = 0$, because we cannot, then speak of quotient c and d.

In the remaining examples, we check the numbers in which the two first and the two last digits constitute two two-digit numbers which add up to 100.

We obtain :

(a) number 9505 - does not satisfy the required conditions (9 is not the quotient of 0 and 5);

(b) number 7624 - does not satisfy the required conditions (7 is not the quotient of 2 and 4);

(c) number 5743 - does not satisfy the required conditions (5 is not the quotient of 4 and 3);

(d) number 3862 - satisfies all the required conditions ($8 = 6 + 2, 3 = 6 \div 2, 38 + 62 = 100$);

(e) number 1981 - does not satisfy the required conditions (1 is not the quotient of 8 and 1).

Hence, Bill's cellular phone PIN number is 3862.

143. The truck needs to make more than one trip to deliver all bulbs to the Xerox's godown. No doubt the truck needs to make atleast one stop in between otherwise the truck can never have enough bulbs left for the comeback journey. And this point needs to be less than 500 if the truck driver wants any bulb to be left when he reaches the Xerox's godown. Let's say it's A.

Philips manufacturing site $\cdots\cdots\cdots A \cdots\cdots\cdots\cdots$ Xerox's godown.

The trick is to make sure that the truck always runs with its full capacity of bulbs. This is true initially as there are total 3000 bulbs and the truck carries 1000 bulbs at a time. So, the truck will make 3 trips with 1000 bulbs to point A. To make sure truck carried its full capacity after point A, we should have a multiple of 1000 bulbs left where all bulbs from the Philips manufacturing site to point A, making 5 trips in between. So, 200 bulbs break in 1 trip. Point A is 200 km from Philips manufacturing site.

Again, we need a stopping point in between A and the Xerox's godown, where there will be 1000 bulbs left after 3 trips. So, the $333\frac{1}{3}$ bulbs break in each trip, point B being $333\frac{1}{3}$ km away from A.

Philips manufacturing site $\cdots\cdots A \cdots\cdots B \cdots\cdots$ Xerox's godown.

In the end, the truck needs to make only 1 trip from point B to the Xerox's godown which is $466\frac{2}{3}$ km away, leaving $533\frac{1}{3}$ bulbs at the Xerox's godown.

144. Yes, all individuals can reach the other planet! Consider the following abbreviations for the individuals:

F = Federation Officer

A = Alien that can fly the space ship

a = Alien that cannot fly the spaceship.

Then, the flight schedule to reach the other planet is the following

Planet 1	Flight	Planet 2
F F F A a a		
F F F a	--A a-->	A a
F F F A a	<--A---	A a
F F F	--A a -->	A a a
F F F A	<-- A ---	a a
F A	-- F F -->	F F a a
F F A a	<-- F a --	F a
F a	-- F A -->	F F A a
F F a a	<--F a ---	F A
a a	-- F F -->	F F F A
A a a	<-- A ---	F F F
a	-- A a -->	F F F A a
A a	<-- A ---	F F F a
	--A a -->	F F F A a a

145. The smallest possible total is 356 = 107 + 249 and the largest sum possible is 981 = 235 + 746 or 657 + 324. The middle sum may be either 720 = 134 + 586, or 702 = 134 + 568, or 407 = 138 + 269. The total in this case must be made up of three of the figures 0, 2, 4, 7, but no sum other than the three given can possibly be obtained. We have therefore no choice in the case of the first locker, an alternative in the case of the third, and any one of three arrangements in the case of the middle locker. Here, is one solution:

107	134	235
249	586	746
—	—	—
356	720	981

Of course, in each case figures in the first two lines may be exchanged vertically without altering the total, and as a result there are just 3072 different ways in which the figures might be actually placed on the locker doors. I must content myself with showing one little principle involved in this puzzle. The sum of the digits in the total is always governed by the digit omitted.

$$\frac{9}{9} - \frac{7}{10} - \frac{5}{11} - \frac{3}{12} - \frac{1}{13} - \frac{8}{14} - \frac{6}{15} - \frac{4}{16} - \frac{2}{17} - \frac{0}{18}$$

Whichever digit shown here in the upper line we omit, the sum of the digits in the total will be found beneath it. Thus, in the case of locker A we omitted 8, and the figures in the total sum up to 14. If, therefore, we wanted to get 356, we may know at once to a certainty that it can only be obtained (if at all) by dropping the 8.

146. Any route from office to home consists of $3 + 5 = 8$ segments, where the car can move only 5 segments to the West and only 3 segments to the North.

The number of distinct routes is equal to the number of ways of choosing 3 out of the 8 segments along which the car could go North or choosing 5 segments along which the car can go.

Therefore, the number of distinct routes from office to home is

$$^{8}C_3 = \frac{8 \times 7 \times 6}{1 \times 2 \times 3} = 56$$

147. First Definitely Disunited, second Pity City, and third Runaround Rovers. Consider the positional statements. If we have green true (T) and red T, then blue must be false (F), or else no card could have two false statements. Then, red T is first and green T must be next to blue's false positional statement, which contradicts green's true positional statement. If we have green T and red F, we must have green T first and red F third with blue T second to satisfy green's true statement, but that contradicts blue's true statement. If we have green F and red F, then blue must be true, or else no card could have two true statements. However, whatever position blue now has with the other two false statements, it is contradicted. This leaves green F and red T, so red T is first and if green F is to be satisfied, then we have blue F. The red card, is the one with two true statements. If blue's team statement is true, then blue is Definitely Disunited, making green's team statement true as well. But that means no card has two false statements, so blue's team statement is false and green's is true, meaning red is Definitely Disunited (in first place). Runaround Rovers isn't second, so is third, and Pity City is second. (It can't be determined which team is written on the blue and green cards.)

148. Imagine 3 vans (A, B and C). A is going to run round the area. All three vans start at the same time in the same direction. After 1/6 of the circumference, B passes 1/3 of its fuel to C and returns to the police station, where it is refueled and starts immediately again to follow A and C.

C continues to run alongside A until they are 1/4 of the distance around the area. At this point, C completely fills the tank of A, which is now able to fly to a point 3/4 of the way around the area. C has now only 1/3 of its full fuel capacity left, not enough to get back to the station. But the first auxiliary van reaches it in time in order to refuel it and both auxiliary vans are then able to return safely to the station.

Now, in the same manner as before both B and C fully refueled run towards A. Again, B refuels C and returns to be refueled. C reaches A at the point where it has driven 3/4 around the area. All 3 PCR vans can safely return to the station, if the refueling process is applied as for the first phase of the run.

149.

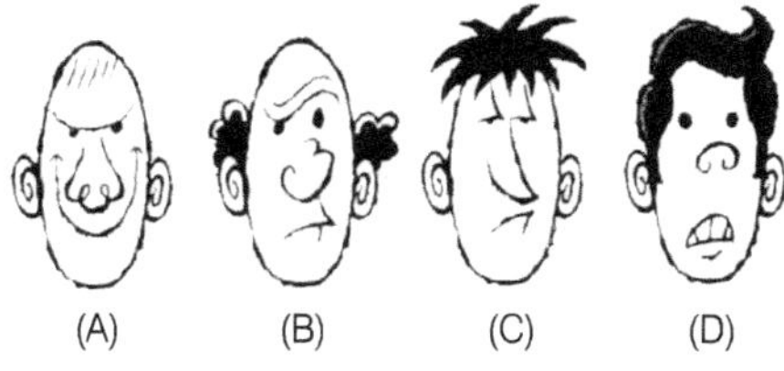

From (3), hair B can be at 2 or 3. If it is at 2 (with nose B at 1 and mouth D at 3), then from (2), mouth A can only be at 2. This means that no item can be correct in the mouth row. If hair B is at 3 (with nose B at 2 and mouth D at 4), then from (1), hair C can be at 2 or 4. At 2, there can be either none or two correct in the hair row (invalid). So, hair C is at 4 (with eyes C at 3). From (2), nose C can be at either 3 or 4. At 3, both nose B and nose C are correct in the noses row (invalid). So, nose C is at 4 (with eyes D at 2 and mouth A at 3). In the hair row, only hair A can be correct (at 1), so hair D is at 2. For the eyes, eyes C are correct at 3, eyes A are wrong at 1 so are at 4, with eyes B at 1. For the noses, nose B is correct at 2, nose A is wrong at 1 so is at 3, leaving nose D at 1. In the mouth row, mouth D is correct at 4, mouth B is wrong at 2 so is at 1, with mouth C at 2.

150. Lynne works in a store (Clue 2). The woman who works in the library was 30 min late (Clue 2). She isn't Doreen or Erica (2) or Claire (4), so must be Marian. The woman with the faulty alarm clock wasn't 20 min late (4), so Claire was 50 min late and the woman who works in the theatre was 60 min late. The woman who is a teacher at the school was made late by the hailstorm (3). The woman who works in the theatre didn't have trouble with her alarm clock (4) and wasn't delayed by strong winds (3) or a fallen tree (5). Thus, she was made late by black ice and (5) Claire was made late by the fallen tree. By elimination, Claire works in an office. The woman with the faulty alarm clock (4) was 30 min late (Marian, above), so Lynne was held up by strong winds.

The school teacher was later than Lynne, so the school teacher was 40 min late and Lynne 20 min late. The school teacher isn't Erica (1), so must be Doreen. Erica works in the theatre.

Thus,

Name	Workplace	Reason	Minutes late
Claire	Office	Fallen tree	50 min
Doreen	School	Hailstorm	40 min
Erica	Theatre	Black ice	60 min
Lynne	Store	Strong winds	20 min
Marian	Library	Alarm clock	30 min